Through D

MW00981413

Entering 2021

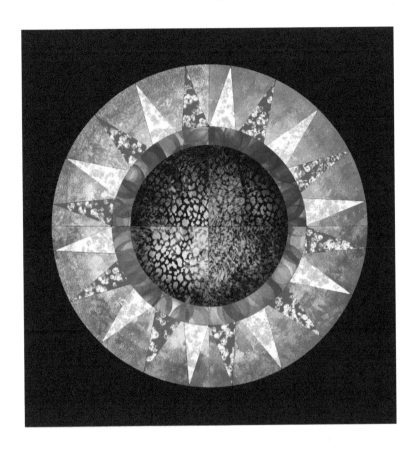

Create with something that's alive.
From darkness create to bring
happiness and light.

Linda Varsell Smith

Acknowledgments

Formatter and Illustrator:
Maureen Therrien Frank
TheMandalaLady.com

Information:
© Copyright 2022
ISBN: 978-1-387-86855-1

Rainbow Communications
471 NW Hemlock Ave.
Corvallis, OR 97330

varsell4@comcast.net

Poet: Linda Varsell Smith

These poems were written during the COVID lock down. Linda is a retired creative writing teacher of workshops and classes at Linn-Benton Community College. Her Literary Publications class produced The Eloquent Umbrella to showcase community writing and art. She was an editor at Calyx Books for over 30 years and served as president of the Oregon Poetry Association. She received the 2020 Pat Banta Award for promoting poets and poetry. She is currently president of PEN Women in Portland. She is a member of several poetry and writing groups such as Marys Peak Poets, Poetic License and Children's Book Writers. Most still meet on Zoom, but are beginning to open up. She belongs to Writing the Wrongs to Rights huddle formed from the Women's March. Linda is an avid cooperative and competitive Scrabble player–just meeting again. She likes plays, most poetry readings, art, craft fairs and festivals. She studies astrophysics and diverse spirituality. Linda lives among over 3000 angels, Swedish folk art, elves and fairies, seasonal felt miniatures in her mini-museum with her husband of over 60 years Court. She likes to escape quarantine in the backyard to gather chi and to go on weekend rides with Court. They do not get out of the car. She has lived in Corvallis, Oregon, Oregon for over 50 years.

Through Darkness Lightly Contents

Quotidian Experiences

Excursions

Contemplations

Natural Phenomenon

National Focus

Global Events

Cosmic Connections

Quotidian Experiences

Out with the Old. In with the New.

2021 starts with an abundance of advice
how to maintain an aging body and uplift
spiritual and creative vibrations.

In the midst of a vomiting virus
on New Year's Eve, the new year
did not appear to begin on a high note.

All the advice and attempts of elevation
were nil. I was flushing and stretching
abdominal muscles, trying to catch overflow.

I was exiting the old and very careful
what I ingest of the new. The heating pad
was not working very well. Strange sounds.

Low energy. Just felt rotten. What a way
to greet the new year. It is fitting to end
2020 this way and purge its uncertainty.

Not in the mood for resolutions or writing
anything new. So I work on editing and
sorting the sections of my book Curves.

I find another heating pad as I coach
my body to relax and try to heal. In this
pandemic I seek home remedies.

Chicken noodle soup. I even pass
on dark chocolate. Somehow I want
to hope and cope this new year.

Scams

This Sunday we had 14 scams
from Olivia for Apple claiming
someone's in my iCloud account.

We do not even own any Apple
products. The calls came from
different local phone numbers.

Some of the numbers were
people's names, some companies,
some just said Corvallis.

The message was computer
generated. Olivia sounded
the same on all the calls.

You could not respond. Perhaps
if you listened to the spiel. I heard
Olivia and hung up. I tend to pick up.

My husband sees an unfamiliar number
and lets it ring its five times. I am afraid
I will miss a local call I want.

He thinks they will leave a message
if he ignores them. At times calls
wake me up and five rings is jarring.

This morning three calls clustered
around 9:30 a.m. Hubby noted the
three calls were other scammers.

We have had several hours now
with no new scam calls. We can only
block 25 calls and we get more than that.

Whoever invents a scam preventing system
will be very rich. All the cooped up pandemic
scammers have us trapped.

Musing Under Covers

A diffusing contrail feathers,
blends with clouds in blue sky.
Leaf-shine on the holly leaves.

Our meticulous mower finds
wily ground cover to mow
in mid-January.

The front yard arrays large
patches of sun amid camellia,
holly, myrtlewood and juniper.

A window frames the view.
I snuggle under warming
covers. It is cold outside.

My schedule is flexible.
Nothing is urgent.
I can rest and speculate.

I miss sitting in the backyard,
but I am a fair-weather friend.
The sun is nice to see, but

I am not lured outside to either
yard. All looks tranquil, but
a facade for much turbulence.

I find I skim the newspapers,
watch less TV news, skip emails
for the words are harsh, fearful.

I prefer to cocoon in blue blankets,
hope for elusive sleep with strange
dreams, perhaps real elsewhere.

Getting a Moderna COVID Vaccine

In Corvallis we were to go to OSU
Reser Stadium East Concourse.
This was for 1a group–mostly
over 80. Younger care givers were
also serviced. We parked in a
handicapped spot near Gill Coliseum.

We were given instructions on-line
to go to certain gates and follow
the signs. On the plaza outside, our
temperature checked, then another
table for green hand band and
a blue ticket. We were bundled up.

Both of us had gloves, hats, layers.
I had a lap blanket. It was not warm
for the first stop inside. We handled our
forms we had from on-line, picked up
further instructions, credentials checked.
We moved on to several tables for a shot.

After my shot, which did not hurt, they
ran out of shots at my table. Several
other tables held up green signs for more
vaccine. He found a table for his shot.
His was painless also. Then to the side
tent with chairs six-feet apart for 15 minutes.

I found a floor heater and put my wheelchair
near it. No one in the group we were in
indicated any reactions and symptoms. We
were told when we could go to the next stop
to make a follow-up appointment. She had
some computer problem and asked for help.

Finally we both had 11:55 on February 25th.
Court navigated the whole experience deftly.
We left home 10:30 for an 11:15 appointment.
Frost in the morning. How much traffic unknown.
As we left we saw lines-six feet apart waiting
for the first entry. We were lucky–no waiting.

We grabbed some lunch from Arby's en route
home. I was anxious before we went. We were
still unsure whether we would be in cars.
I wondered about people without computer
skills. Publicity and information could have
been better, but the process worked quite well.

All the long-lines on TV were not here. We
were familiar with the campus, but I was
concerned about others. Handicapped access:
good. So I hugged my blanket tight, wore short
sleeve tee and sleeveless vest for vaccine access.
Not to move right arm to get vaccine in blood.

We join grandson and son who received their
shots through work. After essential workers,
teachers and assisted living facilities–the over
80 for two days at Reser. We all wore masks
as required and kept our distance. But inside
the open concourse, it was still very cold.

So far no symptoms. Two hours out I will
finish typing and take a nap. Oregon is facing
a downturn in infections and may downgrade
from extreme lock down soon. Schools locally
could open the end of March. I hope enough people
will protect others with safety precautions.

Ode to Mothers

"I feel like a ticking time bomb that is being pushed to the breaking point, but then I am able to defuse myself. Goodness, this is taxing." Dekeda Brown

Mothers during the pandemic are tired,
angry, exhausted by working and mothering.
Cooped up, on-line jobs, desiring
more support, day care. Heavy load smothering.
Some single mothers are overwhelmed and
so are married mothers left in command.

Angry, exhausted by working and mothering.
Schools closed. Someone's left home.
If they can, work at home, some employers not bothering
Mothers leave work. Support would be welcome,
some see their employees have childcare access.
Mothers balance family safety and need to progress.

Cooped up, on-line, desiring
a break, financial subsidies, release of anxiety.
Many find themselves aspiring
to find relief from their sexist society.
Some mothers are at the brink
and do not know what to do or think.

More support, day care. Heavy load smothering
un-leases mental health crisis adding to race,
poverty, special needs children...frothing
at the obstacles mothers face.
Acting as care-giver, teacher, wage earner—
higher level jobs, social security on back burner.

Some single mothers are overwhelmed and
frustrated by fears of not paying bills.
Mothers are not getting services they demand.
Will fewer women have children, avoid standstills?
There are moments of generosity and joy
from helping others and those they employ.

So are married mothers left in command?
Marital status still raises child-rearing questions.
How can partners balance roles and understand?
Who is providing assistance and suggestions?
Women need to roar a primal scream
and have their slice of the American dream.

7

Trying to Nap

Snuggled
in warm blankets,
I take an afternoon
nap. I try to calm my swirling thoughts.
Restless.

Birds chirp
outside window,
leap to holly berries
to camellia, petals falling
like snow.

Wind gusts
sway branches
with erratic rhythms.
I turn my back from the window.
Focus.

My thoughts
are chaotic.
Too much contemplation?
Quarantined from some effective
action?

Relax?
Listen to tape?
Sometimes sleep is no balm
to calm. No blanket can keep out
the chill.

Becoming Anti-Social?

No meetings or events to host or attend.
No table for snacks as we critique or play.
I miss my family and my friends.
We meet on screen, Zoom— a non-touch way.
Social distancing. Masks conceal.
Waiting for the full reveal.

No table for snacks as we critique or play.
We gathered for Scrabble spread off board
across the tablecloth in a haphazard display.
We critique poems by Zoom, still not bored.
We still can chat, but in our allotted time.
Write in free verse, forms or rhyme.

I miss my family and my friends.
We're cooped up, cocooned at home.
We wait impatiently, hope pandemic ends.
Any contact with others is welcome.
We're hug-deprived, eager to touch.
We didn't realize how much.

We meet on screen, Zoom–a non-touch way.
We up our tech skills to participate.
Back in contact for as long as conditions stay,
to share with others what we create.
Play is an element when we get together.
Word-play in common, our bonding tether.

Social distancing. Masks conceal.
No bad breath, fewer facial imperfections.
Patterns on masks now appeal.
Fashion takes new directions.
Communicating at a distance less impact?
Fake news, consensual fact?

Write in free verse, forms or rhyme.
Word play energizes spirit and soul.
Do not expect to contact the sublime.
Play a distant, but connecting role.
We are social, but under new conditions,
caught in a whirlpool of new transitions.

Scammers

Scammers have their victims captive.
With so many in lock down, they hear the call.
Some phones identify numbers and you can hang up.
But their incessant calls wake you up.

Whether is too early, too late or during a nap,
sleep is disrupted whether you answer or not.
Interrupted sleep increases stress and
causes health issues–a real nuisance.

I am sure people do this for a living,
but their livelihood irritates many. I do
not want to string them along, so I just
hang up. Some have ways to avoid them.

Apparently some services can prevent them.
Numbers change for scammers and people
you do want to communicate with. I do not
want to mute or turn off the phone.

I have yet to receive a scam call from a product
they pitch that I want. Don't call me, I'll call you.
Overwhelmed by unwanted emails as well. My
delete finger is tired. My hang up hand annoyed.

Second COVID-19 Shot
    February 25th Reser Stadium

The sun shone as we head to campus
under the stadium seats, ground level.
Crocuses line the route, ready to burst yellow.

Abundant volunteers guided us into lines
under tents to register. The lines moved
smoothly and at 11:30 they were short.

At three tables we confirmed our names
from second shot list, received a red sticker.
Finally we moved to tables 13 and 14.

We received our shots and moved to a
holding area for 15 minutes. We had 11:57
and 11:58 as our release time if no problems.

I was bundled up in my wheelchair with two masks,
warm hat over ears, which also held mask bands
on my wimpy ears, a jacket and red cape.

The red cape covered my body shoulders to feet.
I was toasty waiting. Everyone was very pleasant
and helpful. When we returned to the car,

rain speckled the windshield while we were inside.
Tiny white robots roamed campus like mobile
toilets, to deliver hot and cold food. We saw three.

At a drive-thru to pick up lunch, crocuses start
to poke yellow blooms amid bark dust. Perhaps
dandelions will bloom like sun rays soon.

Any attempts to bring light into these dark times
is welcome. Yesterday our great-grandson was born.
Things are brightening and lightening up.

Finally Daffodils

Though it is still blustery and cold,
the daffodils open sentinels of spring.
The power is out, traffic lights snarl
the traffic en route for a massage.

I did not wear a hat, my hair flung
as if it was electrified. I stayed outside
just long enough to go inside chilled.
Then no heat inside. No heated stones.

Some pads retained some warmth,
but it was the massage which kept
me from really being uncomfortable,
not the thin sheets. She was moving.

I was a slab of flesh sandwiched
between thin covering and table,
usually nice and toasty. We kept
thinking the power would come on.

My husband went back home for
the hour and our power was just
15 minutes out. I ordered a hot
lunch through a drive-thru.

Apparently our power grid is
woefully inadequate. Oregon
generates abundant energy
to export it to other states.

Driving home I thirsted for color–
the color combinations on homes,
daffodils blooming in yards. Somehow
it made me feel more hopeful.

A Trip to the Dentist

As I rolled into the office
I noticed no one else
was in the waiting room.
Chairs are placed about six
feel apart. My double mask
keeps jumping off my wimpy ears.

An assistant takes my temperature,
squirts sanitizer on my hands while
I wait for my teeth cleaning. Another
assistant guides me into the preferred
stall and takes my blood pressure.
It was not too high to delay service.

The dental hygienist arrives in full
white garb with a mask and face
shield. She picks plaque, attaches
an air purifier to the bright light.
She looks like an astronaut: all
the equipment like a surgical room.

My hat, coat, purse and mask are
placed on a nearby bench. I close
my eyes from the light. After she is
finished poking my teeth the dentist
arrives in face mask and shield.
All so sterile and white.

He does not find anything to make
more money off of me until I should
return in September. I put on my
accouterments and roll to the waiting
room. When I entered with my mask and
hat, only my eyes were seen to identify.

Soon my hubby arrived from watching
a Zoom funeral. The timing worked out
fairly well. A call from a friend made
me feel less anxious before I napped.
Perhaps by September, things might
open up and we'll be a little less up tight.

Greeting Our Great-Grandson

We are 81 years older than our
great-grandson. Last cared for
an infant over 50 years ago.
Our youngest grandson is 25.

He is an adorable, tiny baby
with the mighty name of Achilles.
With his chock of dark hair his
expressive face, tugs your heart.

Cradled in his mother's arms,
nursing or sleeping, his tiny
fingers sleeved and feet wiggle.
A beloved new family member.

From his parents he received
a diverse DNA inheritance. Native
American, Ecuadorean, English, Scotch
German, Norwegian, French for a start.

His good looking parents cuddle
a beautiful son. I may only see him
for a few years before I depart, but
I will treasure every moment.

Double-masked, social distanced
I dare not risk holding him. Double-
dosed with vaccinations, still might infect.

In a few months, we can gather family,
hug and celebrate little Achilles, for now
we try to keep everyone safe.

Lock Down Companions

In my bubble is my hubby
and thousands of miniatures.
My clothing is a tad scrubby.
Walled in. Outside obscures.
   Screens and lack of contact.
   My schedule is very compact.

And thousands of miniatures
on surfaces and walls—
angels, folk art, seasonal creatures.
Shades closed from cold, rain squalls.
   I amble around room to room.
   I neglect chores and vacuum.

My clothing is a tad scrubby.
Tee shirts, sweat shirts and pants,
makes me look even more tubby.
   Socks on feet I shuffle about,
   sweeping floors clean no doubt.

Walled in. Outside obscures.
Windows frame what I can view.
Searching solutions for what cures
all the dilemmas in my purview.
   My heavy thoughts weigh me down.
   I try to uplift in world upside down.

Screens and lack of contact
bring information, connect with others.
People at distance attract
desire for hugs, disconnection bothers.
   My screen companions must do for now.
   This pandemic will end someday, somehow.

My schedule is very compact–
empty days without medical appointments.
Curtailed meetings of writers, to be exact
along with Scrabble, no outside art–a disappointment.
   Phone calls soothe a little bit.
   As for exercise? I'm much less fit.

Getting Ready to Zoom

While we are pent up for the pandemic,
Zoom allows us to attend meetings.
We can mute, shut video of ourselves,
extend distant greetings.

My writing groups can show their work
sometimes email in advance
so we can print out to critique,
give each writer a chance.

Zoom brings events we can't attend.
The codes can be unwieldy, complex.
The camera quality varies wildly.
We stand to stretch and flex.

Being a name in a black square
is like email with sound.
I like to see faces, reactions,
whether silly or profound.

When on Zoom I wear a hat.
My haircut is long overdue.
My bangs droop over my eyes—
wild, straggly shag, an unruly hairdo.

People design backdrops—
mine a bookcase with files and books.
Rather bland, I prefer colorful.
Not pleased how it looks.

With my computer and high tech,
I expand my curiosity and explore.
I can connect, give virtual hugs.
I join the world once more.

Hoppy Easter

Easter traditions change with COVID.
For the second year celebrations change.
We no longer can do what we did.
Our approaches rearrange.
       Hoppity bunnies or stuffed ones
       get a view on screens and cell phones

For the second year celebrations change.
Church services move outside or on Zoom,
trying for a healthy exchange,
social distancing for more safe room.
       Some people seek a vaccine.
       Others avoid, endangering scene.

We no longer can do what we did.
Our family Easter parties hoped for sunny weather
to hunt for moneyed eggs, baskets slid
in hiding places brings family together.
       Easter gifts for all ages.
       Fun for all engages.

Our approaches rearrange.
This year we will not celebrate
except Easter dinner for three, so strange
to stay home to recalibrate.
       We exchange greetings by email,
       phone calls and snail mail.

Hoppity bunnies or stuffed ones
won't be bought by us this year.
No baskets, money plastic eggs atones.
Any soft rabbits would bring cheer.
       Maybe a bunny will hop into our yard?
       I would have to hope and imagine hard.

Get a view on screens and cell phones
how others manage to gather.
I'll be one who postpones.
For me, I'll watch. I'd rather
       wait until the sign for all's clear
       before I'll bring Easter here.

Haircuts

Last summer Tani Wu came to my backyard
to cut my hair during lock down in my chi chair.
It was warm and sunny. Shorn white hair floated
to the ground for birds to soften their nests.

I was a stalk tossing fine strands or an animal
shedding fur in this soothing season.
We wore masks. After the clipping, bangs
did not obscure eyes, I felt lightened.

Now in late March, Tani came again, but
it is chilly. Both masked still, he cuts my hair
in the dining room. Hair fans out on the floor.
No doubt I have gone completely white.

A friend found a hairdresser who would come
to homes and assisted living centers. He has an office
as well. Some steps hinder a wheelchair. I have not
been in a store for a year. Both had two COVID shots.

The hair is vacuumed after he leaves. He works
hard to layer and makes my fine, sparse hair bloom.
If I tried to cut my bangs they would look gnawed
or lockstep soldiers lined up for review.

It was also my 81st birthday, Tolkien Reading Day,
too early in the morning. I have a massage ahead.
He admired my collections, especially fairies and
angels. I sit amid angel feathers plucked from spines.

Next haircut, it will be warm. We will still be masked
in lock down. I will not wait as long. I want the birds
to get my hair clippings, not a bulbous vacuum cleaner.
I'll think of my hair as a white cloud amid held at bay gray.

At the Post Office

Today we mailed five overseas books
to Isle of Man, Sweden and New Zealand.
Lots of paper work to process.
Five books for $132.25.

Tomorrow we will bring the domestic
batch, less expensive, less paperwork.
We can drop them off in the morning
and pick them up later in the day.

I sit in my wheel chair to sign some slips.
Notices: "Stop whining. $5 fine."
"Unattended children will be given
a red bull and a new puppy."

One young father wanted to buy the
stop whining sign. Short waits for
the other clerk. I watch and wonder
what the masked ones looked like.

Customers come in with boxes and
envelopes, buy forever stamps.
The masks are colorful. On the floors
are circles to indicate social distance.

One old women came in without a mask.
She left it in the car. She covered her mouth
in embarrassment. She apologized. Around
her, floral and plain masks conceal identity.

It is hard to identify masked faces. Speech
is often muffled. People you know may change
hair color or style. Eyes are everywhere.
In line I watch the parade to the glassed counter.

The postal staff are pleasant and efficient. My
order of mailing envelopes came in two days. We
hear about postal problems, but here we do not
seem effected. It took 25 minutes to mail them.

All the boxes and postal material on the walls.
One woman in a burka struggled with finding
the right box size and understanding the patient,
courteous clerk. I hope the box she bought fits.

The postal center is in a hot tub, pool gear
place. Customers bring purchases to another
counter. Almost everyone is polite, masked, social
distance observant–a respite from turbulence.

First Foray into the Backyard
    April 16, 2021

At 2:22, an auspicious angels number,
I venture into the backyard to sit
under the mossy, budding hazelnut tree.

I did not carry my blue pillow for the black.
metal chair. Bottom, the concrete angel
lolls on his back on the small blue table.

I place my iced tea beside the mini-yellow
tennis ball Bottom cuddles under his arm.
Above me Airlika, the rusty angel wind-wiggles.

Wind chimes vary tempo with the wind.
Tootsie, the weather vane angel is still
in the garden with an erratic pinwheel.

No dog barks next door. No neighbors
out this warm, mild, 70ish day. For me perfect
to inhale chi and rattle my chakras.

Two apple trees begin to bud white and pink
blooms. New branches arrow sky with tiny
bud-lets beginning to poke through.

Two hazelnuts concentrate on leaf-lets—
like all trees dealing with moss. Pear tree
has white blossoms. Peach tree still skeletal.

I delight in the profusion of dandelions–bright
yellow glow nearly ready- to- let - go puffballs.
Puff your stuff dandelions! I can see you now.

In the garden blue-purple lupin await company.
When the methodical mower lops lawn dandelions,
lupin are out of harm's way, growing strong.

The shed doors are muddy. A few brown leaf
remnants crumble in the grass. The sky is
clear blue. No clouds. A lovely day.

I am walking without my walker. Perhaps
this spring I will heal. My broad-brimmed hat
protects my nose from skin cancers.

I can wear a mask as a nose protector also.
Today I am social distanced, alone in the yard.
Four white butterflies and no-see-um bugs fly by.

Oregon's Song: Oregon My Oregon

Amy Shapiro rewrote J.A. Buchanan's lyrics.
Still sounds archaic, racist and over the top.
Still uses Hail to thee, but overall better.

From Buchanan:
Land of Empire builders/Land of the Golden West
Conquered and held by free men, Fairest and the Best.

From Shapiro:
Land of the Majestic mountains, Land of the Great Northwest
Forests and rolling rivers, Grandest and the best.

In the second verse:
Blest by the blood of martyrs
Replaced by:
Blessed by the love of freedom

refrain update::
Hail to thee, Land of Heroes/ My Oregon–now
Hail to thee, Land of Promise/ My Oregon.

Who is fairest? Why celebrate violent, deadly
encounters. Who are the martyrs? This
song from 1920 still could use some tweaking.

Fortunately I never sang this song as much
as I love Oregon. Where is the desert and ocean?
Where is celebrating diversity?

They argue the song reflects the time period
and the writer's intention. That time has past.
Perhaps someone will compose a new song?

Until the song reflects all the current Oregon
experience and is more inclusive, I record my
own Oregon experience with love— aware of flaws.

Scrabble in Sunshine

After months of no Scrabble game—
four of us manage to muster
for a backyard game. COVID to blame.
All have their shots—a lock down buster.
        Several players could not come.
        Those who could, a warm welcome.

Four of us manage to muster
to play in partial shade.
Closer than social distance we cluster.
With rusty diligence we played.
        We rotated board for each turn.
        I hoped my nose wouldn't sunburn.

For the backyard game, COVID to blame,
we wore hats and most of us masked.
Outside safety was our aim.
to protect each other, we were tasked.
        Many months of catch up,
        now that we match-up.

All have their shots–a lock down buster.
Some feel comfortable to be unmasked outside.
I remain a COVID distruster
I kept my mask on and complied.
        How long will restrictions remain?
        Still en force when we meet again?

Several players could not come.
Several in and out to commitments, so
situation became worrisome.
The game was interrupted by come and go.
        Some friends hug, brought brownies and flowers.
        A delightful way to spend a few hours.

Those who could, a warm welcome.
I came early and left early too—
a respite from pandemonium.
It was an enjoyable thing to do.
        I eagerly await our next meeting–
        hopefully with a warm, supportive greeting.

Feed the Bees

Pardon the weeds. We are feeding the bees. Laura Lahm Evenson

Beside the backdoor is a sign
which says Pardon the weeds.
We are feeding the bees.

I sit under the hazelnut tree
Puffballs grow, blow fluff–
wafting gently to a green landing.

Yellow dandelions do not seem
as much of a feeding station as
apple blossoms whose petals fall.

The apple tree is beside the hazelnut,
so I can see the bees jostle
the petals which float gently into grass.

When I move the chair for more sun,
rusty metal angel Airlika has a dried pod
on her back. She sways calmly.

Under filmy, thin-cloud sky the sun
remains strong, but it is still chilly
without my red cape. I shiver.

I thought early afternoon the weather
would be warmer. Birds shriek
and chase each other–don't perch here.

Four white butterflies do not land.
No dog barks. It is quiet, peaceful.
Things seem so normal.

We are a pesticide-free yard. The wind
chimes jingle. The pinwheel spins.
Grass splotchy with buttercups.

Spring brings births and deaths. COVID
continues its global tragedies. I cannot
grasp it all. Deep breathing, energizing chakras

does not release the pain and despair.
What can I do to support the future?
I can feed the diminishing bees.

Staccato Sunday

On a Sunday mid-afternoon
I listen to the intermittent bird
song from several kinds of birds.

A hummingbird hovers over blueberry
blooms. A blue jay briefly perches
on the top of the fence, back to me.

My neighbor passes by the fence
without seeing me. White butterflies
spurt from our yard to his yard.

A dog gives two barks, but several
squeaks from a chewy toy. Three
planes fly overhead, lost in foliage.

Each day the azaleas and rhododendron
redden with more blushes. Four buttercups
compete with dandelions near my chair.

Still some lingering leaves from fall,
crunch and flake into the grass. The
puffballs release more seed.

Wind gusts rouse the wind chimes and
pinwheel spin. The yard angels pause
between swaying. They get plenty of rest.

I remember my hat, jacket and blue pillow
for this short foray into color and calm. If
only my mind could be so tranquil.

I leap thought to thought, unsettled.
Constant change within the flow.
Connect-disconnect struggling to know.

Calm Before the Wind

Midday is mild and balmy
in the backyard. By late afternoon
it was cooler, windy and overcast.

Beside me is the only dandelion
left and only a few puffballs after mowing
of lawn's beard six days ago.

Clouds billow. My blue pillow flattens
thin on the chair. Airlika, the hazelnut
tree angel is shaded and still.

Dogs bark ardently. Sirens and wind
chimes mute. White butterflies
are few. Bluebirds fly into the yard.

One bluebird poises on the fence. Two
chase each other across the yard.
Three dig for worms in the bark dust.

Yard angels Tootsie and Bottom just
hang out–maybe napping with eyes
open. Any animate angels remain invisible.

I know the date from reading the morning
newspaper, as my daily rituals are the same
and blur which day it is. Still in lock down.

My backyard chi and chakrah sessions
help me confront our current situation,
breathe deeply and exhale suffering.

This morning I had a call that a mutual
friend is losing her grip and moving. So sad.
She was so brilliant, I hate to see her dim.

I ponder the world condition — all the
pain, disease, unrest, unkindness.
In my colorful backyard, I can find peace.

The flamboyant azaleas and rhododendrons
lure the winged-ones. Their blooms spark my
spirits as a bluebird nips a small strawberry.

The green hose coiled in the green grass
was straight yesterday. Perhaps tomorrow,
moved to a different sprinkling spot it'll meander.

A Balmy Mid-Afternoon

After a long Saturday ride and short nap,
I slip on shoes and pillow my backyard chair.
My Andean hat protects me from warm sun.

The warmth feels wonderful on my back.
I have buttercups on both sides of me. I face
the erratic pinwheel. Wind chimes behind me.

Butterflies fly mostly solo. Just two circle
each other–not touching. Most do not even
land, but some have brief floral landings.

All totaled they're probably not a kaleidoscope.
All totaled our trees probably would not be called an
orchard. But the stacked sidewalk chunks could be a wall.

A hummingbird lands on a blueberry branch.
Whirring wings grab my attention. Seven scrub
jays–one by one grub in garden bark dust.

Tiny cheeps in the rhododendrons wait for food.
The scrub jays disappear to become hidden in
the bushes. Airlika angel shines on the hazelnut limb.

Tootsie, angel weathervane and prone Bottom are as
motionless as I am. I chuff chakras and deep breathe
chi. The mower is about to lop yellow flower heads.

The dandelions are extinct in the backyard. The
buttercups seem able to duck the blades. White clover
might be low enough. I go inside so I can't see slaughter.

Warming Up

Two days before June, after a massage,
I head to the backyard to warm under
a robin's egg blue sky. Only a few breezes.

I check on the irises, buttercups, fruit
and nut trees as well as swelling azaleas
and rhododendron–all in various stages.

Small green apple nubbins blush when
facing the sun. Too big for birds to gulp,
but growing for larger creatures.

The scrub jays poke around and as I
was getting up–a jay swooshed right
by me, followed by third white butterfly.

Soaked in sunshine, I went inside
for a nap, legs up and lymph flows.
I was in my warm, cosy bed–when

I am startled awake by a voice on a
Zoom call. I am not pleased. I debate
to toss the blanket or hold it tight.

I decide to go to my computer and
warm up my mind and fingers in a poem.
I watch a friend's recorded Zoom reading.

It is time for dark chocolate and to focus.
Like a blurry pinwheel, a rattling wind chime
my mind's at the whim of the windy muse.

Waiting for Summer

The wind barely rustles the wind chimes
or spins the pinwheel. Clusters of clover
and batches of buttercups expand their sprawl.

I sit under the hazelnut tree as shadows
wax and wane, sun sporadically warms my back.
I have dark chocolate pieces in my pocket.

No butterflies today. Bee nuzzles several
clover beside me. White fluff floats and
falls, nestles in the lawn and on stone.

A scrub jay flies into the hazelnut canopy,
tail spied beyond branch. The bird jumps
to the ground—gorgeously blue– and flies away.

Later a second scrub jay imitates the first.
A strange bird call in the distance. Large
dark birds fly above like silhouettes.

More flowers crumble and shed petals.
I thought spring brought them and kept
them until autumn. Guess not.

I need my jacket, but tepid sun makes
hat superfluous? I look forward to playing
Scrabble later–inside, unmasked.

We are emerging slowly from lock down
like spring releases summer. I miss most
the dandelions. Buttercups just not as radiant.

As COVID restrictions lessen, we are still
vulnerable. I am cautious when I leave
the safety of my backyard and its inhabitants.

Expectations

Minutes after I went into the backyard,
carrying my pillow and wearing my hat,
the sun broke through the gray clouds.

I was expecting a day like yesterday
chilly, moody shifts from shade to cloudy.
But sun sustains and shadows reign.

It is mid-afternoon after a lunch with
family members, carrot cake and ice
cream to top off make your own sandwiches.

I was full, deciding between chi chuffing or napping.
I hoped I picked the best time, before rain
appeared. My floral friends welcomed me.

The buttercups flutter in shivery wind.
Iris and rhododendron white petals fall.
Stretching white clover hold their heads,

while dandelions have left the scene.
Not even a puffball. Azaleas peak
and curl. Lavender rhodies hold on.

Two monarchs fly near me, their dark
edges contain translucent yellow panels.
Two white butterflies leave the yard.

Sun penetrates my thin jacket to warm
my back as I hoped. The wind chimes
are vigorous as is the pinwheel.

We have a new wind chime to put up
to add to the cacophony of birdsong
which is absent today. One silent jay

pecks in bark dust. Where are all the sights
I have grown to expect. Summer has arrived
leaving spring changes behind? I miss absence.

Book Gathering

I am rounding up books for our great-grandson.
I have many books from teaching Children's Literature.
Most of the books went to our collector son.
I want books to go where they'll be a treasure.
    I have many books still for all ages.
    I own thousands of pages.

I have many books from teaching Children's Literature.
I hauled them to class in boxes on a hand truck.
They were heavy, I felt cautious and insecure.
How I did not get hurt is just luck.
    The books were sorted into categories
    to go with lessons and type of stories.

Most of the books went to our collector son.
He has collected children's books for years.
A new sorting of few left has begun.
I want some to go to great-grandson, it appears
    I'll have to signed him up for Imagination Library,
    which I did, but no delivery yet to beneficiary.

I want books to go where they'll be a treasure.
Grandson remembers us reading to him.
He's eager to read to son as he comes more mature.
I am searching for books I kept on a whim–
    old favorites remain, spark poems and memories.
    These books are creative emissaries.

I have many books still for all ages,
Clearing the shelves will be a task.
Books to meet many developmental stages.
Pass them on is all I ask.
    Great-grandson is only a tad over three months old.
    I hope he'll enjoy what he's being told.

To go with lessons and type of stories,
I have some tapes for a later date.
He'll build his own depositories,
I hope he will appreciate.
    I cull my shelves and plastic bins.
    My books' new adventure begins.

Sitting Outside in a Heat Wave

Today it's predicted to reach 110.
At 10:00 it is 86. Wimpy gusts tingle
wind chimes. Weathervane Tootsie–dormant.

En route in the side yard, a neighbor has
a lush patch of puffballs and dandelions.
I pause to admire them over the wooden fence.

I sit in hazelnut tree shade with Airlika, rusty
angel slightly swaying above me. Wide-brim
hat and blue pillow accompany me.

I sit among clover, face east. An intricate
spider web on a thread connects branch
to branch, snags a bug. Sun shines on the web.

The gardener with his small plastic bucket
picks blueberries–enough for a few days.
He waters the peach tree and roses.

Somehow leaves cling to the sickly peach tree
and a few peaches begin. The lichen covered,
scrawny tree survives unlike beloved cherry tree.

Butterflies circle dance. No bee lines to each
other. From different directions they dance.
and take off in different directions again.

Even in the shade, the air feels heavy. It
is not a comfortable sit. Petals look rusty
before they fall. Bark dust smothers weeds.

I go inside. We are shaded and buttoned up
to conserve air-conditioned cool. The pandemic
keeps me inside mostly anyway.

I pity the withering flowers and browning grass
with no escape from the incessant heat. We are
not alone. The world heats up with us.

Blue Lights

Four blue candlelights in two windows,
a necklace of blue lights rim the front door,
blue bulb in the lamp post through winter months.

Small, calming, guiding lights through
a dark time. Not red or green to stop or go.
Blue–warm, my favorite color, welcoming.

When the ordinary white lights return,
they will brighten the night, but not
my heart, as the blue lights do.

So when skies are cold and dark,
I can peer out the windows and
gaze at the blue sky lights and smile.

Few visitors, but travelers on the road
can drive by, recall Christmas and
the festivals of light, if but for a moment.

Lock Down Companions

In my bubble is my hubby
and thousands of miniatures.
My clothing is a tad scrubby.
Walled in. Outside obscures.
> Screens and lack of contact.
> My schedule is very compact.

And thousands of miniatures
on surfaces and walls—
angels, folk art, seasonal creatures.
Shades closed from cold, rain squalls.
> I amble around room to room.
> I neglect chores and vacuum.

My clothing is a tad scrubby.
Tee shirts, sweat shirts and pants,
makes me look even more tubby.
> Socks on feet I shuffle about,
> sweeping floors clean no doubt.

Walled in. Outside obscures.
Windows frame what I can view.
Searching solutions for what cures
all the dilemmas in my purview.
> My heavy thoughts weigh me down.
> I try to uplift in world upside down.

Screens and lack of contact
bring information, connect with others.
People at distance attract
desire for hugs, disconnection bothers.
> My screen companions must do for now.
> This pandemic will end someday, somehow.

My schedule is very compact–
empty days without medical appointments.
Curtailed meetings of writers, to be exact
along with Scrabble, no outside art–a disappointment.
> Phone calls soothe a little bit.
> As for exercise? I'm much less fit.

Three Strikes

Left-side facial shingles
clot on the lung
soft tissue bruise on left foot
Things come in threes and lead
to three days in the hospital.

Somehow we managed to lose
our wheelchair when loading
after the hospital stay. We have
a more comfortable transporter
and the wheelchair is a bit
rickety, so finding it was not urgent.
But the lost and found located it
a few days later and we picked it up.

Daily the facial pain lessens somewhat.
I have no idea what the clot situation
is doing. My bruised toes are sore.
I have no idea how these ailments
found me. I am quarantining myself.
The pandemic in Oregon surges
along with wildfires.

I go outside going to doctors. We take
weekend rides but I don't get out of the car.
My typing is still slow and wonky. My bone
on bone knee cream helps some. I need
to be more mobile. Perhaps my knees is
malady #4 so my three strikes didn't
take me out.

Back to School

Yesterday the masked students
and staff returned to refurbished
classrooms. The younger ones
are not vaccinated. For their own
reasons some of the older ones
are not either.

My children and grandchildren
have aged out. Great- grandchild
an infant. One is in college
and vaccinated. Somehow the message
you get vaccinated not just to protect
yourself, but other is not stressed enough.

The world with its wars and sickness
must seem a scary place to children.
It sure is to old folks like me. I wear a mask
willingly. Some of my masks are fun
and some carry a message. I have
colorful fabric masks and Ruth Bader Ginsburg.
Masks actually improve some faces.
I wonder if youngsters think masks are
removable parts of the face? A fashion
accessory? It's true mission will become
known in time. How long this masking will
be needed is unknown. Just make the
best of it and be creative!

Afternoon Respite

On a balmy, fall afternoon
my husband tells me we have
a deer sleeping under the apple
tree in the backyard.

I go to the window and see
a buck with just sprouting
antlers. I watch him sleep
until he goes into the garden.

He napped behind a fat trunk of
an apple tree–I see nose and
wagging tail. He gobbles leaves
apples, fruit, berries voraciously

Then a second deer- a doe
emerges from the bushes. She
was camouflaged so well I did not
know she was there until she moved.

The buck caught his emerging antlers
in a tree branch trying to eat leaves.
Several times he became entangled.
The doe just watched the predicament.

They are about the same size. She
leaves the yard first. It takes a few minutes
for him to follow. I enjoyed spending
a half hour in the company of deer.

My husband will close his deer gates
he designed to deter deer. I am glad
he had not gotten to that task and I
could bask in the beauty of deer.

Dealing with Shingles

Pain effects left side of my face.
Reading and typing worse than usual.
Shingles is the most painful of
all the recent maladies: clot on my
lungs, falling down twice, three days
in the hospital. Was shingles to blame?

My muse went on vacation, not wanting
to inhabit this unbalanced creature.
I stayed inside most of the time
except for a weekend ride. Then I
stayed in the car. Laying down on my bed
is still the preferred option.

For a while fudge delighted my taste ,but
when I ran out: Dove Dark Chocolate.
A physical therapist came with her
zillion questions. Many seemed
irrelevant to my condition and gave
me exercises that are easy for me.

This quarantine broke for an outside
Scrabble game. Our son visits.
Our Salem gang is Zoom or phone.
My great-grand-son Achilles grows
older picture by picture. Someday
I can hold him—until too heavy.

I am in limbo. Writing projects delayed.
I wait for my recovery and needs from
others. I throb with lower-level pain
and sore body. Look forward to naps.
I want to live and give again. How much
longer must I wait to move forward?

Excursions

First Sunday Drive of 2021

Our mission was to go to Salem
to deliver Christmas-delayed
salmon from Astoria on a sunny,
clear, beautiful wintry day.

En route to Salem a brown squirrel
just escaped becoming road kill.
Masked people walk and bike.
Women mask more than men.

We had two stops- daughter
and grandson households.
Our son-in-law had some
of his fabulous fudge left for us.

Our grandson had a brief break
from work for the exchange and
a chat. At Carl's Jr. we encountered
three seagulls shining in sun.

East toward Silverton–many tree farms,
forests, fields, wineries, winding hilly
roads. Oregon rolled out its lush beauty
with a glimpse of snow-capped Mt. Jefferson.

In Silverton the vintage houses never
cease to charm. Somehow leaving
town we made some questionable
turns and turned to GPS for guidance.

To me it is a miracle how Samantha
not only can map a route but also
give verbal instructions. Due to a few
days of intestinal upheaval, I stayed in car.

So I remained cooped up in a car, instead
of our home. I really did not mind. I knew
I was still sick when I could postpone
devouring the fudge for a day or two.

Glowers

On a drive we saw a parade of power towers
strewing power lines across the road, above
a field and over a hill. The skeletal obelisks,
latticed for transmission lines scar the landscape.

Some call them Electricity Pylons but most
agree they are a form of visual pollution.
One in Florida is shaped like Mickey Mouse,
but these are ugly, metallic monsters.

Can we add some artistic flare? Turn them
into glowers–like show-ers or growers, not
flowers or hours. The diamond-shapes
could dangle crystals to dazzle in the sun.

They could emit rainbows. Or vibrant stained
glass panels. Solar panels could even
provide night lighting? Sprucing could provide jobs.
Artists and craftsmen could design the panels.

A mosaic. A mural. Digital displays. The possibilities
are endless in creative hands. Birds add dots of
color as they rest. Perhaps some nests attached
to the towers for aerial dwellers? Hanging Gardens?

Towers become sculpture. Some places have
gigantic lines to transport. Artistic billboards?
Perhaps if enough people object to their presence,
and are not turned into art, all the lines will go underground.

Ride into the Wild Ways
    January 10, 2021

The fog lowers and lifts, clouds thicken
and thin, sun peeks and hides as we
ride up highway 22E toward the Cascades.
Logs pile along the roadside with clearing
debris from the September wildfires.

Along the road especially near the towns
of Gates, Detroit and Idanha, concrete
foundations filled with trash from former
homes and buildings. Burned evergreens'
trunks torched at various heights.

Scorched patches beside unscathed swatches.
Two houses nearby had different fates.
The fire danced its fire dance in a frenzy—
choreography from a mad terpsichore.
Fires crossed the road. Many trees then axed.

Big Cliff and Detroit dams lowered the reservoir
for winter snow melt. Stumps and boat ramps
go nowhere. A devastated landscape
revealed— more scalped than the fire- ripped
forests and families. Some RV returned.

Car chains clot from slow drivers– rubbernecking
or mindful of curves. Miles and hours of forests
with dots of human intrusion. Some power lines
snake along the side of the road. The piles of
logs and debris escalate. How to recycle them?

Abruptly we had snow on the roadside, going
and coming. Snow crept up snow poles. Cinders
on the snow and road. Moss-covered bark with
light-green branch beards of moss dangle.
The snow tainted with cinders, dirties cars.

At Santiam Junction we took 20 back.
This valley did not have the fires and
remained intact and lush. Some rural
poverty as we drove to Sweet Home
for a quick lunch. We escaped rain.

But we did not escape witnessing
the damage to the environment fire
left in its wake. Clean up begins.
Heartbreak continues as people
excavate what is left of their dreams.

Fog, Fire, and Snow

We left the Willamette Valley
in fog. As we climbed into
the mountains, fog lifted
and sun cast shadows on the road.

We followed the South Santiam river
which did not have wildfires. Lush moss
on Douglas Firs, hemlocks and other
evergreens towered above the road.

As we neared Tombstone Pass, snow
covered with cinders, lined the road. We
saw snow-capped Three Fingered Jack,
but roadside had less snow than last week.

On our return we followed the Mackenzie
River, saw Three Sisters glistening. Both rivers
gnash white caps on riverteeth, fill several
reservoirs and dams for electric power.

The chunks of lava displayed sporadic snow.
The lakes were low to absorb snow melt.
Then the fire patches began. Mill City and
small towns like Rainbow so many scorched trees.

Logs pile beside the scenic byway and burn
in bonfires. At first I thought fog returned.
Miles after mile of concrete foundations
filled with the remnants of fire and brick chimneys.

The fire jumped the road- leaped over some
dwellings beside ruins. RV temporary homes
as dwellers did clean up. Blackened trees
and stumps scar the landscape for miles.

Snow zones came and left abruptly. The
fog returned to the valley. For a while the sun
warmed us in a green and gray scenario.
As we approached Springfield–garish signs.

The winding mountainous roads straightened
out on I-5. Overcast skies, but no rain. Images
of soft moss on giant trees, fire damage
dancing down the byways until exhausted.

Rural Ride

Our Saturday drive to less congested areas
was sunny, cold and a bladder-ful long.
Frost lingered beside the roadside.

The upgraded cell phone intermittently
would bleat " loss of service" then "Verizon",
at unexpected places–mostly in forests.

Many evergreens like Douglas fir and
Willamette Valley ponderosa pines line
the roads, some branches wrapped in moss.

The forests were mostly tall second growth.
Clear cuts scarred large swathes. Several
labeled: logged in 2020. Planted in 2021.

We drove through vinyards, forests, farms
which grew Christmas trees, grass seeds,
goats, sheep and cattle.

We drove down Bellfountain road, west
to Alsea, north to Blodgett and Airlie.
amid sun swatches and shadows.

Alsea Falls recreation areas welcomed
hikers, maybe some picknickers. More
traffic than we expected- some bikers.

On a dead-end road to Dawson, we found
historic Hull-Oakes Lumber mill with stacks
of new lumber ready for pick-up.

After weeks of stress and trauma, being
among the lush green Oregon landscape
is calming (except maybe on twisty, curves).

Riding in Sunshine

Snow on the hillsides. Chilly until
the heater kicked in. We are driving
to the Philomath post office to mail books.

Most of the national books were mailed
from Corvallis, but they were having
computer problems and suggested elsewhere.

We had five international, one local
and one box of books for the Oregon
Poetry Collection at University of Oregon.

Sending out the books is a hassle to prepare
for mailing. I welcomed the sun beaming
on the freshly washed, sparkly blue Fit.

Philomath had more staff than Corvallis
and we mailed the books easily. I watched
people mailing in the drop boxes outside.

Three old men and three old women
made deposits on my watch. Lots of
geezers and crones went inside as well.

Many came out with mail from their
boxes. Some younger women came
as well for their mail. All masked.

I did not go inside. Just along
for the ride and company. As usual
I didn't get out of the car.

When we returned to our Covid
cocoon, our trip in sunshine
brightened our afternoon.

Interruptions

On a ride to the coast in
intermittent rain of light and
heavy intensity with sun peeks.

We are breaking free from
Covid lockdown. The cell
phone announces service status.

We enter and exit tsunami zones.
Frothy waves slap shore. Long
drive-thru lines stop and start.

People wear masks or not. We
carry masks near the windshield. He
gets mask entangled with glasses cord.

Homeward we see fire pockets.
Fire leaps leaving homes alone
or destroyed to chimney.

Forest clear cut scars,
blackened scorched trees,
tucked with lush stands.

Remnants of recent snowstorm leaves
thin layer and snow piles, in higher places.
One melting snow man droops.

Cars clump from stop lights and
slow drivers. The traffic is heavier
than we expected end of January.

Some coastal stores are open, some closed.
Mid-March after second COVID shot and two weeks,
then can enter tourist traps and fudge shops.

Then we can plan more than a bladder-full ride.
We can get out to stretch our legs. We stopped once
under a closed shop's overhang to stretch.

In warmer, sunnier times we can get out of
the car, gaze at the sea, spot seagulls, revisit
favorite places, interrupt routines even more.

Images on Ride to the Sea

Two large metal roosters gawk
and a yellow smiley face gazes
at road travelers.

In high passes snow ruffles beside
the roadway. Ciders blackened snow
used by child to build dirty structures.

Gutted home beside rusty trailer
covered by graffiti. Incomplete
billboards. Can not disguise loss.

Calm bays. Roiling sea. Off
shore rocks and haystacks.
Seagulls and a brown speckled bird.

It was overcast, but dry when we reached
Cannon Beach as forecast. I saw school
where I went for two week writing workshops.

We parked at a nearby mobile park. Family leaves
and I will only see them the weekend in between.
I have a chance to explore me and poetry.

Cannon Beach is Portland's
Posh playground. Coordinated
planning. High-end shops.

Cannon Beach has a haystack. Buildings
brown and gray-a cohesive feel.
No drive-thrus. Outside or take out.

Seaside hodgepodge zoning, garish
a touristy vibe. Drive-thrus. Some shops
offer trinkets and souvenirs. Some closed.

We were surprised there was so much
traffic. It is February. Masked people
stroll in chill. I go outside mid-ride to stretch.

Leaving in bright sunshine. Light to heavy
rain most the trip. Windshield wipers swipe
dribbling rain patterns on the blurry glass.

Valentine's Day Flatland Drive

Due to rain, snow, strong winds north
of us and in the hills, we chose
a flatland, Willamette Valley route.

Corvallis was in a pocket- just escaping
northern and eastern storms. It was
raining lightly and cold.

We did not get out of the car and
headed south toward Eugene. As we
left a squirrel tight-roped a power line.

Flocks of small black birds landed
in the fields. Sheep and cows rather
than towering evergreens.

In towns on a Sunday and due
to the pandemic, many places
were closed and people scarce.

We were uncertain of directions
under gray skies. We finally got
out GPS Samantha, sought gas.

Daughter and grandson and partners
went to the coast yesterday and found
snow and a tree across the road.

Court researched open roads Some
had snow. Today they checked in.
Grandson staying another day.

Worried about the family and stress
about gas, I sought relief with dark
chocolate candy for Valentine's Day.

When we arrived back home, I took
a nap. Do not remember any sugar-
coated dreams, but delicious memories.

Uncertain Skies

Gray and white clouds bunch
above us on our ride south—
sometimes rainy, sometimes sun.

My sunglasses went on and off,
until I just let them stay in place.
Wet ditches, roads and green fields.

We went down the valley between
the two mountain ranges. North
is still thawing from recent storm.

We chose from three routes.
Soon we were rural with red,
five-pointed stars and flags on homes.

One home had a large sun symbol
which seemed a good idea for Oregon.
Paint and upkeep on homes varies widely.

Horses wore blankets. Lambs and
cows were left in the cold with newborn
lambs and a calf scampering about.

There was also a llama farm. Small
towns with white, charming churches.
Newer churches lacked older ones' style.

One farm stacked tires, covered them with
white plastic, added top hat and a face for
a snowman. Most signs and decorations down.

We stayed in the car and ate at DQ
in Veneta. Stores did not have much
traffic even in diverse malls.

One school had a wistful sign to students
saying "We miss you". Mostly things look
normal, when they are uncertain as the clouds.

On a Sunny Sunday Drive

We left Corvallis at 11:00 and
head toward Florence on the coast.
Newborn lambs and small calves
dotted the farms. Small towns
had white churches and Dollar
Generals. A perfect prelude to spring
day. Forests with moss-covered
limbs and trunks as if wearing
green coats. Traffic moderate. Most
people outside wore masks. Green
and lush fields and evergreens.
Christmas tree farms and fields
readying seeds. Birds on wires
when they could rest in cushioned
comfort on branches. Wineries
have moved south from north
in the state which they claim has
4,500,000,000 trees on forest land.

We did not get out of the car in
Florence, but people milled around
and ate outside. Many dogs on a leash
with mostly masked walkers. Clouds
that bunched in the valley, vanished
to clear blue skies over a blue-green
aqua sea with frothy waves. No seagulls.
We found a candy shop open in Seal
Rock that sells delicious fudge. Court
went inside and found dark chocolate.
So smooth and creamy. It was Sunday
so not sure if some shops are not open
on Sunday or closed by pandemic.
The waves crashing on the rocks,
haystacks and beaches– a vast horizon.

We drove along 101 to Newport
before heading inland back home.
Bikes and motorcycles shine in sun
Cocooned in the car we discussed
memories from our youth. We wondered
what happened to those long ago classmates.
We enjoy the familiar roads and places.
The sun blasts warm through the windshield.
At the height it was 58 nearing home.
Things looked so normal, except for masks.
We returned home from Newport at 4:00
at our bladder limit. We both rested for
about an hour. For a few hours we are
outside time and stress. The cars bead
up as if a necklace with missing beads.
I feel so grateful to live in beautiful Oregon.

March 1, 2021

Another sunny day. Still in lock down.
Yesterday we drove along the coast.
We entered and left tsunami zones,
sometimes very quickly.

The cell phone chirped "loss of service."
Then "Verizon" when it returned. The
blips and signs changing unexpectedly
distracted us, No respite from inland.

The waves glistened then pummeled
rocks and sand. The shops did not
appear as welcoming as months ago.
The coast used to be a crowded, breezy place.

Despite balmy skies, I am not calmed.
Outside the window: sirens, traffic sounds.
Birds rest on branches, but I am unable
to nap. When awake I feel fragile.

With daily assaults from the news,
connections limited to on-line. A dental
appointment tomorrow and other medical
appointments do not lift my blues.

The phone rings, the computer requests
responses. Screens do not compensate
for in-person touch. Disruptions. Meditation
in the backyard weeks away.

My moods swing from celebration with
the birth of first great-grandson, to despair
at the suffering around me. I'm off-balance.
Whatever the weather's within me, I'm swirling.

Cloud-Followers

We head north on our Saturday ride.
Four hours under an ever-changing sky.
Billowy, white cloud sculptures mix
with banks of gray clouds bearing rain.

We drive up the valley with wide vistas,
of flat farm land, orchards draping
moss-covered trees with loped off limbs.
We are not able to detect what fruit will bloom.

Two bonfires burn branch debris.
Roadside and forest areas have
fallen trees from an ice storm. Limbs
litter the ground. Fields are greening.

Alpaca and cattle graze. Tree farms,
wineries, vineyards, ranches add
to rural diversity. Small towns with
Dollar Generals and pot shops.

Many closed stores and restaurants.
Hubbard hosts a Hop Festival. Canby
is a garden spot. Rain spritzes on
and off, most heavily on last leg home.

In our car cocoon we can discuss our
concerns. We do not use GPS, but
his cell phone for directions. No sound.
I was on alert for turns. We use drive-thru.

I drape my mother's red cape over me.
When sunny, the heat beats through
the windshield. We keep on our sunglasses
and the world looks lush.

Clouds fascinate both of us. The panorama
stretches for miles. We try to define
images in the mountainous clouds.
Both of us enjoy their natural beauty.

The world floats and expands when you follow
clouds. Earthly issues abate for four hours.
We drift with the clouds and our spirits lift
in light-shifting sky. Dark birds fly below.

Campus During Lock Down

We drove on campus to pick up
a pre-ordered book from the closed
library. Only a glassed window
pass-thru access on showing your card.

Hibernating books wait to fly off shelves.
A few employees roam the stacks.
Dusty books only looked at when requested.
Research mostly done on-line.

Like going to a bank wearing a mask
like a bandit. We drove by locked and
dark buildings. Only some places
will open. Most classes are on-line.

A few masked students walked in
the light rain. They social distanced
when encountering each other face
to face. One student biked.

Mostly it looks like a deserted city.
The once bustling campus will
not fully reopen until fall. Nearby
food sources do not let you inside.

Little white robots like square lunch
boxes carry food to students dwellings.
Many dorms are not hosting students.
Top-heavy daffodils droop in the rain.

To the Sea

Mostly sunny skies meld into
gray by the coast. Trees bloom
white and lavender/pink.

Stacks of branches beside
the roads from fallen trees
during recent storms.

A few daffodils, but not wild flowers.
Some green buds sprout from
the trees. Shadows splat the road.

Most of the curves en route have
been straightened so the ride
is easier to navigate.

On the coast we found Indulge
the Seal Rock sweet shop and
fantastic dark chocolate fudge.

We go in and out of tsunami zones.
His cell phone voices our status.
Some interludes are very brief.

We drove Corvallis, Newport, Seal
Rock, Waldport, Corvallis amid
moderate traffic. Long lines at drive-thrus.

Most stores are open, but we must mask
and social distance. I am not lured to
go inside any store. I miss craft shops.

Masked people walk dogs and stroll
arm and arm. Craggy rocks froth waves.
Patient people wait in lines to eat in cars.

More traffic on the coast. We are moving
into spring and soon summer when restrictions
should loosen up some–we hope.

Coming home cows graze in lush green
fields. Houses–humble and grand line
the route— well-spaced amid forest.

When we leave the valley for the turbulence
of the sea, somehow the ocean scrubs
the shore. We breathe deep and exhale fear.

Vernal Equinox Views

A ride to restore balance, change
and renewal this day with sun then rain.

Sometimes windshield spritzed with light
rain and then, windshield wiper swish.

Wild and cultivated daffodils line
roads, glow in yards and fields.

Seven flocks of black birds ink
the sky with wavering patterns.

We are on lush verdant scenic byways,
mostly rural with fields and forests.

Spring lambs romp. Cows munch.
Horses glisten in sun, shine from rain.

I am concentrating on spring blooms
instead of house paint colors.

We route around bigger towns for
smaller two-blinks communities.

We had GPS and his cell phone when
we were uncertain of our path.

We headed south to Coburg, to Sweet
Home, Lebanon for late lunch and home.

Most people inside. Many shops closed
as well as restaurants. Drive-thrus active.

I am wrapped in my mother's red cape,
cuddled and warm on this uncertain day.

I wear a hat to keep errant overgrown
bangs out of my eyes. Days until a haircut.

We are still in high risk lock down. I look forward
to going outside unmasked. I want to sit and inhale chi.

The dandelions await my admiration—
dots of sun to guide us into spring.

Drive to Tillamook and Cape Meares

We drive north and then west
on the Trees to Sea byway.
Sun warming the chill through
the windshield, sanitizing masks
on the dashboard. Perfectly clear day.

Most of the trip is forests and farms,
wineries and cideries, clear cuts
and lush forests–some old growth.
Clear cuts wound the hillside, leaving
stumps to decay in rain and sun.

Someone built a fence of stacked logs,
all the same length about three feet high
rimming the yard, easy access to firewood.
Another yard had a fence of painted old
bicycles- lined up and linked in rainbow colors.

Farms and orchards. Trees not in bloom and
unlike some clear cuts give no dates or what
they are growing and with clear cuts two said
replanted in 1998 and 2016. Japanese cherry
blooms white, flowering plums- lavender.

Daffodils in abundance, forsythia started,
no Scotch broom. Dairy cattle and chickens
with rural folks out in short tees mowing
and tending to their acreage. Cell service
bleeps in and out like with tsunami zones.

No political signs up. Some yellow smiley faces.
One smiley face on a hillside amid a clear cut.
Some crows, no seagulls even on the coast.
One royal blue bird with black top knot. Traffic
heavier than we thought to and fro.

A sign for Horses Healing Hearts and Love One
Another. The town folks walk dogs. Hikers and
bikers out in force. Some restaurants and stores
have open signs–but require masks. Some churches
welcome Easter visitors tomorrow.

Several roads to Cape Meares closed. Finally
we found one with access. We encountered
several dead ends and had to turn around.
The ocean frothy and air too cool to get out
of the car. As usual we dined drive-thru.

The conifers are always so lushly dark green.
The deciduous trees still gray-brown, barely budded.
Many blooms yellow and white. The flowering
plums appear an apparition. It is emergent
spring. Maybe next week we'll reach 70 degrees.

Winter ice storms broke branches. Skeletal
limbs pile beside the road. Swatches of forest,
blown over, gouges in green. Some trees protected
by towering conifers. No wildfires' debris noticed
on today's routes, but plenty of downfall.

I am so eager to sit outside, celebrate dandelions.
Some escaped the Fisker hand mower, lying low
in the cut grass, some lopped heads composting
the lawns–but some feisty survivors will bring delight.
I peer out windows and hope for warming.

Lured Toward the Sea
April 11, 2021

On a cloudless, chilly sunny day,
we head for the coast–Newport
to Florence amid moderate traffic.

The coast is beautiful on a bright day,
even when we have almost freezing
mornings with high 60's afternoons.

Frothy, foamy sea flattens as the
waves hit the shore. Dark rocks
block the waves. Trees slant inland.

Heading to and from the coast,
deciduous trees remain skeletal,
only a few hint at budding leaves.

Many trees are coated by moss. Some
dangle scruffy beards. Wineries and
orchards too early to identify, unless told.

Sporadic clusters of daffodills,
and clover. Japanese cherry trees
bloom white, flowering plums, lavender.

Woman and her dog on the side
of the road, vaguely smiling
with a tepid wave.

At the fudge shop a crow drinks
from a dirty pot hole beside the car.
No seagulls seen. Few other birds.

Some businesses are open. Tourist
shops and some indoor dining. All require
masks. Signs indicate if open.

We do our usual stay in the car
drive-thru. Long lines. Some cars'
rear ends are in the roadway.

Heading inland, thick forests , clear cuts
and lopped branches. One stump had
a sign saying 275 years old.

On the Applegate Trail, cattle
and wobbly-legged spring lambs,
romp, nuzzle and graze in sun.

We looked at the clock and it said
333–the angel number for pouring
power and energy into us,

Also the number for joy and playfulness,
finding one's spiritual calling and your
life purpose. Sounds good.

When we arrive home, a neighbor
across the street is cutting down
a tall magnificent redwood.

The tree limbs are stripped with
a Christmas tree high in the sky.
Horrible screams from a worker.

Our trees block the scene. Not sure
what happened, but many people are
there to help him. We are near a hospital.

All's quiet now from the front yard. The
sky is clear blue. My mind recalls the
gray-green sea and tugs me to visit soon.

Drive to the Ocean
    Via Blodgett, Summit, Siletz Reservation, Toledo, Newport 4/17/21

We left 80 ish valley heat for 50ish foggy sea.
Everything so lushly green, emergent.
Small daisies, daffodils, flowering trees.
Life flows. Nothing seems urgent.
        We do not get out of the car.
        This works for us, so far.

Everything so lushly green, emergent.
Dense forests, clear cut screens.
Varying replanting dates are evident.
Branch debris from recent storm scenes.
        Shade over the road cools our ride.
        It is so warming inside and outside.

Small daisies, daffodils, flowering trees—
swatches of Scotch Broom starting.
White, pinkish, yellow blooms in breeze
wave as we are departing.
        Gravel road seems out of place
        and rumbles our comfy space.

Life flows. Nothing seems urgent.
A flattened barn, rusty roof,
weathered boards, rustic element.
Unattended, isolated, aloof.
        We pause and take it's photo
        from a cell phone in our auto.

We do not get out of the car.
Drive-thru a DQ. Some shops open.
Tourists clog sidewalks, unmasked ones jar.
Business is booming. Bayfront thrives again.
        The fog rolls in, obscures the shore.
        We head back to the valley once more.

This works for us so far
to protect public and ourselves.
No matter who you are,
Now you need mask yourselves.
        All the beauty still surrounds us.
        Reminders for all that grounds us

Marys Peak to Pacific Scenic Byway

Our destination was Walport. Out of overcast
valley through the Coast Mountains
to coastal sunshine. In front of us
in the gas line was a black Trump truck

with signs on its rear end like "Hunting the
original fast food under a rabbit","Run the woods."
On the tire a flag and "We are all one together".
Bear paw prints in the back red lights.

One barn en route had "Don't tread on me"
with a flag. Along the bay from Toledo a shop
was called Holy Toledo. More people stroll
historic district amid rapid development.

Some walk masked, some not. I wanted
to wave a mask out the window at them. Most
unmasked were men. Women protected others.
We could not detect smiles- just eyes.

North of Waldport was Indulge the sweet shop.
We bought the last seven pieces of dark chocolate
fudge, a three day cookie for Court and ice cream.
I thought we'd be too far North to visit.

In Newport traffic was heavy. People oblivious
to COVID guidelines stroll the stores. Kids flew
kites. Beachcombers picnicked and walked
dogs on the beach a low tide.

In Nye Beach we drove by the yellow and green
Sylvia Beach Hotel where I spent many days with
writer friends. Each room has a different author theme.
Now my knees balk at the stairs. No elevator.

In a park stands a tall metal angel with mismatched
wings. Both of us wear matched shirts with matching
masks of the cover of my book "Grounded with Gaia".
My shirt concealed under my red cape.

All the drive-thrus had long lines. We rotate places,
eat in parking lot. I get a kid's meal and save
the toys for visiting children–few these days.
When new normal returns, there should be many.

Driving home through farms and forests. Clear cuts
look like bald heads with fringe. Calves wobble. Scotch
broom sweeps roadsides. Flowering trees. Beautiful.

Back home, images from the ride recall moments
in time to imprint into poems. More open signs
each ride– flashes of hope and healing.

Approaches to Fitton Green

For our Saturday ride, we explore three
entrances to Fitton Green Natural area,
where my husband and a friend like to hike.

It is a lovely forested area west of town.
New housing encroaches. Clear-cuts,
replantations, old growth, near by.

We had about a three-hour drive
by grass seed, mint and meadow foam
farms. Cattle overlooking Scotch broom,

Queen Anne's lace, mysterious small
yellow, white and lavender wildflowers—
lush leafy, needly, green everywhere.

On a Philomath detour we saw a man
sitting in his garage with wooden bird
houses and trees. The foot-long trees

are made of at least three kinds of trees.
I've seen them at craft fairs. We stopped and
I found just a perfect one for my collection.

After driving to the three trail heads, we took
a forest road into a wilderness area and luckily
finally found a map at a state park.

We meandered to Dallas where we found
lunch. All the drive-thrus at two had lines.
We had plenty of time to decide what to eat.

It was sunny when we started out but became
overcast. Masked people mostly. Elderly gardeners.
Traffic heavier than usual as people escape lock-down.

We went today instead of Mother's Day tomorrow.
Traffic could be heavier. But many mothers could
lighten up when the drive is to see them.

Repeat Ride to Walport and Backyard Retreat.

Late morning under cloudless blue
skies we wend our way on Highway 34
to the lightly foggy sea.

Bikers, hikers and motorcyclists lured
westward along with fairly sparse traffic on
shadowed roads, attracted to scent of the sea.

Scotch broom, lupin, azaleas, Queen Anne's
Lace in full bloom drape the edge of the road..
Homes tucked in the forests. A few birds.

When we arrive at Waldport, we head north
to Newport. The fudge shop is closed due
a family emergency. We found another shop.

Masked and unmasked people stroll
in town and fly kites on the beach.
Some restaurants are open inside.

Drive-thru lines are long. People get their
cars in line and crawl forward. The coast
will build up traffic from now on.

Returned home via Highway 20, it's not
as curvy as Hwy 34. Sections have
been straightened. Tree branches

from winter storm pushed awkwardly
off the road. Lots of free fire logs
for the industrious to pick up.

Late afternoon I retreat to the backyard.
Limited breeze to spin the pinwheel,
clang the wind chimes, sway the yard angels.

I sit under the west hazelnut tree and face
Airlika the metal, rusty, angel with patina.
She shines in sunspots between leaves.

In the garden a puffball nurtures a yellow
dandelion. Buttercup battalions from both
ends of the yard march toward each other.

Tootsie, the gray weathervane angel
permanently toots her horn northwest—
more a statue than helping us know wind.

An ant hikes up my walker, climbs on
the concrete angel Bottom, while another
crawls through grass. I am ignored.

Along the fence the azaleas and rhododendrons
flamboyantly display fully open blooms.
Like on our ride, the floral bouquets delight.

Trip to Sisters: Burn and Chill
    5/22/21

We leave the valley and head
for the Cascades- up: Hwy 20.
Down: Hwy 26. Scenic byways-indeed.
The skies became clearer en route, until
cloudless when we came home. The majestic
snow-capped mountains are worth the trip.

Under bright overcast skies, enhanced
by sun-glasses, soon we see the devastation
of wildfires. Salvage logging piles logs
and brush on the roadside. Gray skeletal
trees and stumps, tiny trees trying to grow.
Acres and acres, miles and miles of burn.

Fog engulfs us near Tombstone Pass.
Plowed snow rims the road. Patches
of snow tucked in ditches, spread under
trees and open spaces. Mostly conifers,
but some mixed forests. Burned out homes,
ash covered foundations and chimneys.
Little new construction but log removing crews.

Big equipment to clear the logs and debris.
They create traffic chains of around 30 cars,
letting one side go at a time. Approaching
Sisters is a huge mall as large as downtown.
Very stucco with some wood accents— ordinary
for the convenience of tourists.

We have traveled this road and visited Sisters
for decades for skiing and small craft shops
with log cabin feel store fronts, unique artwork.
Now mostly book stores, quilt and antique shops with
polished storefronts. Gone the quaint, quirky days—
vivid hippies conforming, commercialism now forefront.

It was crowded. Crawling through town. Hard to park.
We went to the mall area for drive-thru lunch. We were only
one in line, then cars line up. You could dine-outside as
passers-by are masked—or not. Social distanced—or not.
No idea who is vaccinated—or not. We did not get out
of the car-as usual. Time to head down the mountain.

B and B plus Holiday Farm wildfires scar the landscape.
More demolished homes. No fog or snow to chill. It was about
50's in the mountains-up to 71 in the valley. Over 250 miles
of up and down, I'm heartbroken over changes, dwell on
memories of a lush forest and a town whose changes disappoint.
Glad it is not winter, summer or Memorial Day weekend.

Rural Ride to Veneta

Memorial day weekend we take our ride
through less-trafficked rural roads. Fields
and forests, farms and clear-cuts.

The wildflowers are in full bloom–Scotch
Broom, white daisies, tall Queen Anne's
lace, dandelions and orange poppies.

One clear-cut hillside was carpeted in
Scotch Broom, yellow blooms rim
the road and cluster on open areas.

This is their time to mirror the sun.
Filmy clouds, few contrail scars.
A gorgeous 70s spring-summer day.

The line at the DQ in Veneta was
sluggish. Customers had few other
options except Mexican fare.

Lots of bikers and walkers–mostly
masked. Some stretches we were
alone, shadows over the road.

Large clear-cut patches–one replanted
2014. We could guess by the height
of replacements how long since logged.

Any dwellings we see are mostly very
well-maintained. Tiny towns barely bulges
from the road. Bare essential services.

In one town a small white church with blue
trim was for sale. It would make a cosy
community center for gatherings–someday.

Driving to Corvallis we see many fields
of fescue, ready to harvest and send
much of it to Japan. Strawberry pickers.

To hold masks, maps, napkins, tissues
on the dashboard from migrating, we will
look for a low basket with suction cups.

The ride lifts spirits. Then I go to the backyard
to ponder the local scene with anticipation,
without the sunglasses left in the car.

Under-Equipped Observer

To recall images on rides and sitting in backyard,
I decided to use a notebook to record what I see.
On our ride the notebook stayed on the dashboard.
When I went in the backyard, I left it in the car.

In the car I wear sunglasses which perks up color.
In the backyard in bright light I yearned for shade.
We did not get out of the car, but had walker with us.
At home I carried the blue pillow to chair without it.

In the car I wore a jacket, but did not need it.
In the backyard I left the jacket inside. I sit
under the hazelnut tree, beneath rusty angel
Airlika. She needs a dusting on her back.

Saw one butterfly on our road trip, but here several
flit about. Two duos circle each other and fly in
different directions. Two scrub jays in the garden
beak-to-beak, then one circles three times.

Like the butterflies they go in different directions.
Solo paths most of the time. Buttercups pop up all
over the lawn. Yellow dots of delight. Azaleas fade.
Rhododendron drop petals. White irises expand.

In the lawn are a few tall grass escapees from
the mower, surveying loped heads and broken
blades. One stalwart dandelion. How can I become
better equipped to deal with loss and destruction?

To the Valley's Edge

We drove across the flat Willamette
Valley admiring the cloud canvas—
a wide vista of all kinds of clouds
as if painted by a brush.

Weather predicted to become wet,
yet the whole drive was dry. We headed
toward Detroit at the edge of the Cascades.
We checked out the wildfire damage.

Certain routes needed GPS assistance.
One driveway was lined in toilets.
Burned homes are being rebuilt. Fire
jumped gaps in a haphazard pattern.

Scorched stumps and timber. Trees
clear cut. Some replanted. Skeletal trees
like shadows of themselves. It is jarring
as they are stacked at the side of the road.

The lumber mills are well-stocked. Lots
of freshly cut boards ready for delivery.
Detroit Lake is low– still boaters and
campers from full campgrounds.

The traffic was medium–bunch and flow.
Small towns with Dollar General, post
office, church too small to support a mall.
Until tourists return, times could be tough.

We saw a fawn on the side of the road, who
turns its head to look at us and dashes into
the forest. The forests are lush conifers
with the deciduous trees less majestic.

Scotch Broom, daisies, big-headed Queen
Anne's Lace and some cultivated gardens.
It hovers about 80 degrees,so the gardener's
and farmers wore hats. Cows look comfortable.

We found gas and drive-thru lunch and started
back from Stayton. Clouds–even with gray
bottoms remain continent. The ride's array of
color and texture diverts one's spirit upward.

Valley to Sea

Before the touristy season on the coast,
we thought we would drive valley to sea
before it became crowded.

Near Philomath we saw four wild turkeys
lining the road, then en route to Newport
three deer stare at us.

Fat-headed, tall -stalk Queen Anne's Lace
more abundant since last trip. Scotch Broom
in swatches, some amid clear cuts.

The brutal clear cuts destroy the lush forest
areas, dark branches shadow the road. Miles
of mossy conifers. Overcast sky mutes green.

Rain sprinkles the windshield. Sun blasts through.
Sunglasses help for it is bright despite patches
of fog and drizzle. Recently summer–50-60 degrees.

We decided to head north from Newport along
the Trees to Sea, Pacific Coast and Three Capes
(Kiwanda, Lookout, Meares) highway.

We go in and out of tsunami zones. Waves crash
outcropping rocks. Few birds in sky, but on rocks.
Frothy sea. Sky gray so sea does not shine.

We went to the Christmas Cottage. You must
wear masks if not vaccinated. I am, but still
wore my mask as we wend wheelchair in aisles.

I tried the walker, but navigating the walker while
browsing and selecting was difficult. Owners say
business is coming back. Down by half last year.

The small, dazzling with ornaments and collectibles
shop, has a limit of 30 customers at a time. We
manage to be under the limit. Ceiling to shelves covered.

I found 8 angels. I have not collected many in the last
year and this was my first foray into a store. I rolled
along enchanted by the creative expressions.

We still dined by drive-thru at Tillamook. Another first
I took the wheelchair into a bathroom at Fred Meyer.
Usually we do not get out of the car. Progress.

We drove through the Grande Ronde tribal
lands with attractive, modern administration
and health care buildings and on Applegate Trail.

Some beautiful stands mostly conifers stretch for
long distances. Traffic moderate. Tree farms many
with dates when replanted —1998 to 2017.

We saw horses, dairy cows near Tillamook
(the Tree City). tree farms at various stages
of growth. Great Christmas tree selections.

We have been over these roads many times,
but every time I find scenes to appreciate.
These lock down rides allow our tradition

to thrive as we explore our beloved Oregon.
In our travels, we have seen many memorable
places, but my heart remains in Oregon

Riding the Heat Wave

This weekend and upcoming week, a heat
wave has been forecast for the Northwest.
Many days over 100–up to 115. We decided
to go on our ride on Saturday.

When we left at 11:00, the temperature
was 79. We rode, without getting out
of the car, south, then west into the Coast
Range as the temperature went up and down.

The high was 104 in Junction City. At home
at 4:30 it was l00. Air conditioning kept car
and home comfortable. In the Douglas fir
forest, shadows cast patterns on the road.

We see campers, fishermen, swimmers,
tubers and rafters on the Siuslaw River.
Many just pull over beside the road.
Mountains look moth-eaten with clear cuts.

The highlight was seeing two black bears–
not too big and not too small scamper into
the forest. A small tree crosses the road.
Wood debris hits fenders. Shadows camouflage

potholes, rough roads, road litter. Lots of butterflies
and strawberry- colored lupin. Vistas are spectacular.
We stopped so he could take a picture. Roman
Rose road was rocky rubble for miles.

We have to turn around. We took suspicious turns
despite help from GPS Samantha and Vera Verizon.
Vera has stretches with frequent power warnings.
At times we seem off Court's plan he worked

so hard on with intricate maps. When we changed
roads, we finally reached a chain of stopped cars.
When we finally were allowed to go, we saw hundreds
of stalled cars slowly begin to move. Very long blockage.

We meandered into the valley and to Junction City
for a late lunch. First Mexican drive-thru was too spicy
for me–so he ate three burritos. We stopped at McD
and I ordered a kids meal. Toy for my collection.

Hay ready to bale, sweats in the sun. Few
animals or people bake in the sun. Driving
toward Corvallis on flat valley floor was a
relief from meandering mountainous roads.

Much of the trip was nerve-wracking with
winding narrow roads, hazardous two-way
traffic, road whales slowing progress. We
encountered traffic at more places than we thought.

As soon as we reached home, I took a nap.
Shades drawn to keep out heat. Tomorrow
will be hotter. I'll have to sit outside early. We
will be riding the heat wave in many ways.

Poetry on the Lawn
    July 3, 2021 Salem, Oregon

During a heat wave under clear sky,
the poets gather on a church lawn.
There is a covered stage for when
the congregation worships outside.

A side-less tent covers the stage and
the mic carries well. The poets huddle under
three tents with no sides for shade from sun.
They bring chair, sunscreen and water.

Few people wear masks. With my floppy-
brimmed hat, sunglasses and mask I am
incognito. Many have not seen each other
in 3-D for 15 months, only on Zoom.

Butterflies and breezes waft through
the tents. Water bottles float in the crowd
of about 20. A cooler is full of ice.
One poet uses it for a foot stool.

We arrive after lunch and open mic about
1:30. We hear seven poets until 4:00. One
poet writes in Spanish and we hear a translation.
To see old friends in person is a treat.

We talk of doing this again and resume our
poetry groups in the fall. Despite heat and
COVID, poets find ways to give gratitude
and share their experiences and hopes.

Wildfires

Mid-July and wildfires rage.
Currently Sisters is evacuated
and in southern Oregon
the Bootleg fire has scorched
240 square miles.

These fires are not expected
to be contained until November.
Heat smoke and fires from these
fires started on July 6th.
Unstable air conditions and extremely
dry fuels make conditions worse.

Power companies inspect high-voltage
power lines to see if they can carry
electricity. 5500 megawatts from Bootleg
Fire disrupted service to California which
has voluntary power conservation 4-9 p.m.

Ash falls down near Sisters.
Central Oregon fires have doubled.
Orange fire retardant, smoke seen for miles.
Ground crews cut fire lines amid grass
and trees. Emergency Conflagration Act invoked.

The state fire marshall can mobilize fighters
and equipment to assist local firefighters.
Three counties called upon. Benton County
is one of them–our county. Scenes of the fires,
orange flames burning structures and forests
are frightening. The valley can only wait.

Contemplations

There Are Times

There are times in this pandemic when
my imagination sets me free.
I can create what can happen.
I can escape in creativity.
> For a few moments I am not cooped up inside.
> My thoughts take me on a roller-coaster ride.

My imagination sets me free.
I draw from dreams and musing.
I ponder life's complexity.
I seek light and what's amusing.
> I'm tired of uncertainty and fear.
> I wonder if certainty will ever appear.

I can create what can happen,
on the page if not in actuality.
With a peck of the keys, slide of a pen
I can create my own reality.
> Poetry lets me succinctly explore
> life's meaning and so much more.

I can escape in creativity
to a place outside of time.
Imagine new places with a proclivity
to express myself in rhyme.
> Poetry has inspired me all my life.
> I am just a words' midwife.

For a few moments I am not cooped up inside.
I sit without boundaries, vulnerable to possibility.
Resisting darkness, to light— I open wide.
Seeking truth is my responsibility.
> People are a disappointment. Planet needs care.
> Poetry's job is to pay attention, make folks aware.

My thoughts take me on a roller-coaster ride:
up and down, light and dark, sad and glad.
I dislike sharp curves, tall heights. I decide
to not ride the roller-coaster, try not to get mad.
> But my moods and insights are hard to control.
> Seems I contend with endless rigamarole.

Fibs We Tell

We
are
alone?
Universe
devoid of other
sentient beings only us?

Some
are
better
by gender,
ethnic connections,
or superficial barriers?

We
are
stewards
of planet.
We face extinction.
Denial, inaction kills us?

We
tell
fibs to
avoid truths,
risk of failure to
meet changes sustainably.

Will
we
act in
time? Preserve
a better future
for descendants? Will we die out?

Consciousness

I read all things have consciousness.
That means inanimates would as well.
Do they all have same senses, awareness?
How are we to know or tell?
        People are deficient in some senses though
        either by birth defects or come to know.

That means inanimates would as well.
The house, furniture, possessions.
My collections observe us where they dwell?
Comments on our indiscretions?
        Do they retain smell in smelly places?
        Can they see if without faces?

Do they all have same senses, awareness?
Some senses less or more acute than ours?
All have feelings for happiness,
no matter how they spend their hours?
        If immobile can they project invisible dopplegangers?
        If they dimensionally shift, that could be game changers.

How are we to know or tell?
We have some curbs on our intelligence.
My unknowing continues to swell.
What do we do better with our sentience?
        Do we all share the gift of life?
        Would knowing reduce strife?

People are deficient in some senses though
other beings may be differently compromised.
If blind, deaf, handicapped we know so.
World more complex than realized?
        Would we act with more care
        if we knew everything was aware?

Either by birth defects or come to know
otherly- abled consciousness is unknown
except in animals and humans, although
I hold out hope all the collections I own
        have found refuge in my home
        and they feel very welcome.

The Love of Form

The love of form is a love of endings. Louise Gluck

I love poetry for its diversity of forms:
syllabic counts, rhymes, breaks of lines.
I love inventing new ones outside the norms.
Word-play is what poetry defines.
      Free verse even has its experiments.
      So many ways to express our sentiments.

Syllabic counts, rhymes, breaks of lines,
create patterns on the page.
The myriad ways a poem combines
to create sound and image.
      Mystery and delight amaze
      whatever current fad or craze.

I love inventing new ones outside the norms.
I collect forms and use them for reference.
I have choices in the way a poem informs.
The poem dictates my preference.
      Each poem invokes my wonder,
      as I explore new ways to ponder.

Word-play is what poetry defines.
Searching for the best word in best place.
Polish until the poem shines.
Find your own audience base.
      Form tells you how a line ends
      and the guidelines on which a poem depends.

Free verse even has it's experiments.
It is not free if it does not communicate.
Free verse contains poetic elements.
A definition is open to debate.
      Since I have a proclivity to rhyme,
      I don't use free verse all the time.

So many ways to express our sentiments.
The more forms you know, the more choices.
Look at form as an opportunity not an impediment
to discovering our own, unique voices.
      I view poetry as mystery, with fascination.
      My way of reaching a goal's destination.

Soul to the Universe

Music gives soul to the universe, wings to the mind, flight to the imagination. Plato

Music gives soul to the universe—cosmic destination.
Music brings wings to the mind,
flight to the imagination.
Best communicator people can find.
> Diverse sounds around the world.
> Intense emotions are unfurled.

Music brings wings to the mind.
Like concept of angels, music of the spheres,
a source of expression for all humankind.
Music is more complex and diverse as it appears.
> I choose upbeat tunes and jazz.
> I can do without razz-a-ma-tazz.

Flight to the imagination,
I composed youthful melodian tunes.
I could not read or write music—a limitation.
Off pitch or off-key my voice croons.
> In college I learned to read music, but
> over the years I forgot, in word glut.

Best communicator people can find.
Globally people listen and relate.
Through musical bonds bind—
dirges or ways to celebrate.
> Never learned an instrument.
> It is a choice I lament.

Diverse sounds around the world
lead to choruses, musicals, dance.
Bands played while dancers whirled.
Rituals and performances enhance
> joy, faith, respite from woes.
> The way the multiverse flows?

Intense emotions are unfurled,
while musicians play.
I am transfixed, mind swirled
as thoughts leap, lets body sway.
> For awhile we are all one.
> For awhile we are not alone.

Prayer

Uncommitted to any organized faith,
I choose to pray to my guardian angel Bella.
Whether or not Bella exists in another realm,
does not really matter. Maybe no being
assists me in this incarnation
but I'd like to think someone has my back.

This is a stressful time with lock downs,
for COVID, extreme weather, flawed
leadership, new ways to protect oneself.
As I wait for my great-grandson's birth,
he is currently en route. Of course I am
anxious for all to go well and safely.

Climate change, political upheavals,
deniers, exploiters bring darkness.
I pray for light, enlightenment, courage.
My age slows mobility, body reflects
my maladies, my energy compromised.
But my prayers are not for me but others.

Prayer is for hope, dealing with challenges
in an uncertain world – a form of comfort
when other ways of thinking disappoint.
Our place and relationship to the cosmos
is still a mystery. Facts vary with point
of view. I am certain about nothing.

Apocalyptic Poetry

Poetry must be capable of answering the challenges of apocalyptic times, even if this means sounding apocalyptic. Lawrence Ferlinghetti

And just how are poets going to answer these challenges?
Are poets visionaries grounded with facts?
Are poets responsible for praises and revenges?
What explanations and solutions for these acts?
      Just how can poets be put on trial,
      when so many remain in denial?

Are poets visionaries grounded with facts?
Whose facts are they thinking of?
Such trauma this concept exacts.
Proceed with sustainability and love?
      For this global belief I offer no clue.
      I am not sure what I believe will be true.

Are poets responsible for praise and revenges?
Poets write odes and dirges.
What are they supposed to do for avenges?
What prompts these poetic urges?
      We have had these challenges before.
      Climate change makes turbulence even more.

What explanations and solutions for these acts?
We've have had several global extinctions.
Cosmic collisions pushed us off the tracks.
Each threat to survival has more distinctions.
      Is the universe hostile or kind?
      These are answers we hope to find.

Just how can poets be put on trial
to bail out humanity's conundrums.
It could take eons. Meanwhile
we will have to twiddle our hopeful thumbs.
      My poems are not bound to any theory.
      I can't address every query.

When so many remain in denial
despite the violent, disturbing scenes around them,
how can we convince the rank and file
to join together in a global anthem?
      Not just poets, but everyone is part of solutions.
      Study diversely what's new, march in peaceful revolutions?

Word-Play

Word-play is my non-guilty pleasure,
Poetry is my preferred expression.
Playing with form, sound and measure,
borders on the fringe of obsession.
       I spoke in rhyme when I was three.
       Poetry is ingrained in me.

Poetry is my preferred expression.
The diversity of choice is full of possibility.
Every word makes an impression
on the reader. I take responsibility
       for each word I place on a page.
       I hope my word-play will engage.

Playing with form, sound and measure,
word by word I compose the line.
The mystery is what I treasure.
The process is hard to define.
       I wake wondering what poem the day brings,
       what questions, arrangements of many things.

Borders on the fringe of obsession,
this poetry fascination in my heart.
I am intrigued with a poem's progression.
The poem wheedles out, I ponder each part.
       I prefer letters to numbers.
       I prefer poetry to prose, laughs to grumblers.

I spoke in rhyme when I was three
My mother wrote down my rhymed quatrains at six.
As soon as I could read and write, my creativity
explored many word-play tricks.
       Now as I am 80 and a crone,
       I find I'm still poetry prone.

Poetry is ingrained in me.
Even my grandmothers loved poems.
I can't imagine living without poetry.
It follows me into all my homes.
       Bookshelves house many poetry books.
       Word-play the lure. Poetry hooks.

Trying to Write a Cheerful Poem

It is easy to get entangled in darkness, when
light seems muted and dim.
We must try harder to be upbeat then?
Our patience reaches the brim.
>   Letters are black against the white screen,
>   presenting a bland, often blank scene.

Light seems muted and dim.
Too many turbulent, foggy days.
Our chances out of lock down are slim.
We have had to revise our usual ways.
>   To see birds, daffodils outside the window,
>   is a gift of light and color they endow.

We must try harder to be upbeat then?
I find dark chocolate calms my soul.
Not into meditation. Back to research again?
I'm trying to adjust to a more constricted role.
>   I miss art, Scrabble, art shows, plays, writing groups.
>   Some on Zoom. Not the same, my enthusiasm droops.

Our patience reaches the brim
when we can see someone, but can not touch.
Haircuts shag and need a trim.
Some things which matter so much,
>   we took for granted last year
>   as we wait for pandemic to disappear.

Letters black against a white screen
express my thoughts, as I soundlessly scribe,
record events never before seen.
Some visions too difficult to describe.
>   My dreams from another dimension
>   make me hope for cosmic intervention.

Presenting a bland, often blank scene–
a computer page seeks color and sound.
I look outside my bedroom window keen
to spot leaf-shine and bird-sheen around.
>   I scan for dandelions–spots of sun.
>   I wish more light for everyone.

When

When will
hope prevail and
despair vanish in air?
When can we breathe free from fear, ails—
ever?

When will
violence end?
Justice, equality
truth, freedom to choose, few isms
prevail?

I am
impatient for
I have little time left.
How can I help before I leave?
No chance?

When will
I know why I
came and what I should do?
Any free will? What limits? Or
puppet?

Do I
incarnate in
multiple dimensions?
How many lives to experience
for what?

When will
I understand
cosmic mysteries and
what beliefs to advocate for?
Discard?

When will
I stop asking
questions, getting no sure
answers? Life's to endure, challenge,
enjoy?

Intolerable Uncertainty

The only thing that makes life possible is permanent intolerable uncertainty, not knowing what comes next. Ursula Le Guin

Le Guin created new realities to contemplate,
creating new concepts of what could be real.
Her imaginative fictional landscape
opens boundaries, new cultures to reveal.
> Some pretend to know what comes next.
> Various dogmas choose preferred text.

Creating new concepts of what could be real
somewhere in the cosmos or invented,
holds endless fascination and appeal.
Any disasters could be prevented?
> Different dimensions and mind creations
> present challenges in other destinations.

Her imaginative landscape
is a fantasy, recreation of future and past.
From this turbulent reality we want to escape.
Change is constant, does nothing last?
> Permanent uncertainty meant for us to probe
> more deeply what we experience on this globe?

Opens boundaries, new cultures to reveal.
We rethink our approaches and choices.
Any certainties we should conceal?
Can we relate to fictional voices?
> Any basic truths in faith or science?
> Any which should command our compliance?

Some pretend to know what comes next.
Some prefer the unknown and surprises.
Some shift opinions and context.
Some just make compromises.
> Some just go with the flow,
> perhaps the easiest way to go.

Various dogmas choose preferred text
and try to convert others to their creed.
Some present a hidden pretext,
to the vulnerable in time of need.
> Oppression, coercion, dominance, laws
> suppress others will and accentuate flaws.

The Helpers

Whatever you do to help may seem very small, but it is very important that you do it. Gandhi

Whatever you do to help may seem very small,
but is it important you try?
Perhaps you think it does not matter at all,
and you ponder why.
        In lock down how do you connect?
        Do you withdraw and reflect?

But is it important you try?
Put on a mask and social distance?
It is too risky anywhere in this country?
Will you face resistance?
        Just what are you to do
        when you doubt you can carry through?

Perhaps you think it does not matter at all,
whether you serve others and mask?
It is not all about you, but while you stall,
many people are not up for the task.
        What are your limits? Frail with age?
        Dealing with illness? Suppressed rage?

And you wonder why
you are on call to help another.
Why are you expected to comply
when others do not bother?
        Are you not up to nurture
        and sustain others in the culture?

In lock down how do you connect?
By phone, deliveries, computer apps?
Is someone else a better prospect?
Are you too drained, disengaged perhaps?
        If it is important you do it
        would you accept it you knew it?

Do you withdraw and reflect?
How long do you stay this way?
It is fear and ignorance, I suspect.
What will it take to sway
        your selfishness to caring?
        Turn your greed to sharing?

Waiting

I am
rambling, rattling
in my COVID cage-home
in high risk lock down for a year,
waiting.

Waiting
to touch, to talk
face to face with no mask
outside or inside protections,
freely.

Freely
on Internet
I connect with the world.
Meetings on Zoom, or postponed, stopped.
Emails.

Emails
keep connections.
Screens and pages inform.
I glean spots of color, diverse
textures.

Textures
to elicit
feelings and touch, bring smiles,
keep senses alive, they're joyous
wellsprings.

Wellsprings
of renewal,
births, seasonal celebrations.
Smaller gatherings when we can.
Waiting.

I Knew an Old Crone
    A Cumulative Poem

I knew an old crone who gulped down a fly
    She did not say why.
        Maybe I should try.

I knew another old crone
    who preferred a scone
        and dined alone.

I knew an old crone who ate a grasshopper
    I could not stop her
        from this snack popper.

I knew an old crone who ate the Easter bunny.
    This was not funny,
        made her twitchy nose runny.

I knew an old crone who chewed a cat.
    Imagine that !
        I smell a rat.

I knew on old crone who did eat a rat.
    Skinned it flat,
        made her fat.

I knew an old crone who digested a dog
    with intestinal backlog
        due to a clog.

I knew an old crone who pounced on a frog
    in her mental fog
        she fell in a bog.

I knew an old crone who caught a kangaroo.
    She made kangaroo stew
        with an Australian brew.

I knew an old crone who confronted a bear.
    She dashed out of there
        with no time to spare.

I knew and old crone who spied a tasty horse.
which made her digestion worse.
No second course.

I knew an old crone who blubbered a whale.
It was hard in inhale.
Fright made her pale.

I knew an old crone who then tried catfish.
Not her favorite dish,
but she got her wish.

I knew an old crone who dined on shark.
Did not light a spark.
What's coming next...hark!

I knew an old crone who swallowed an ant.
In an instant
she was extant.

Love and Fear

There are two basic motivating forces: fear and love. When we are afraid, we pull back from life. When we are in love, we open to all that life has to offer with passion. Excitement and acceptance. John Lennon

During this pandemic, lock down fear
forces us to pull back from life.
We still love, but can't hold near
many we love in the midst of strife.
        I feel I'm in a tug of war.
        At rope's end can I hold on more?

Forces us to pull back from life,
to mask, social distance, don't touch.
Heart stabbed as if by knife,
we wish it did not hurt so much.
        We are observers and isolated,
        not participants, feel ill-fated.

We still love, but can't hold dear
those outside our bubble.
We're still not safe as it might appear.
We dwell in normality's rubble.
        Even with vaccinations,
        many prefer staycations.

Many we love, but can't hold near
are too vulnerable for us to connect.
Guide rules are still not clear.
We step back to reflect.
        It is a time of self-reflection
        and for flaws detection.

I feel I am in a tug of war.
I despair of violent, unjust news,
conditions I deplore.
I want some uplifting clues
        that humanity is choosing love.
        Please give fear a shove.

Not participants? Feel ill-fated?
Many cannot endure the stress
knowing they have participated
to increasing planet's duress.
        Do we have any options to choose?
        Which will win and which will lose?

Trying to Calm

Resting for an afternoon break,
a shadow on my shade displays
two three-fingered bouncing
limbs from the camellia tree.

I watch the wind-tossed branches
lengthen and shorten. I release
stress as I focus on the image.

Spindly, gray alien hands do not
manifest beyond front window into
my room. Shadows are silhouette slivers.

I want to go outside and sit in
the backyard to muse. But it
is still chilly even with sun.

From the car I have seen daffodils in our
 front yard and several batches line the
street. Emergent buds promise spring.

I do not numb in sleep, I remain
vigilant to shadow shifts. Any respite
will be brief as the world oozes pain.

I know then my feet hit the floor I will be
grounded with Gaia and her inhabitants
and cannot escape cosmic connections.

Creating Books

Maureen Frank arrives to exchange manuscripts.
Her blue, green, purple hair is whimsical. She is
a COVID survivor who is getting two shots. She rips
open surprises, an artistic, computer whiz.
            She gave me back Curves. I give her Angels Encore.
            We begin our collaboration once more.

Her blue, green, purple hair is whimsical. She is
an intuitive artist, with a high tech mind.
Imaginative, talented, she knows her biz.
She is the best ally a klutzy, inept computer poet can find.
            We've done about 20 books together with fun.
            I hope our journey has just begun.

A COVID survivor who is getting two shots. She rips
through her symptoms with courage and grace.
She renovates her home and looks forward to trips.
Under her mask there is a smile on her face.
            As I grow older and slow with age,
            she sees my words get on the page.

Open surprises, an artistic, computer whiz,
she creates mandalas under The Mandala Lady,
paints rocks, coloring books, is open to quiz.
With her, color flows cascady.
            Her book covers are vibrant, interior sketches
            also explode as her creativity stretches.

She gave me back Curves. I give her Angels Encore
to format and illustrate as her intuition suggests.
I know she'll find her inspiration as before.
She'll create for our best interests.
            Some people enter our lives to support, strengthen
            our resolve, our goals, as our journeys lengthen.

We begin our collaboration once more.
I move on to another project as she creates,
seeks guidance, explores her creative core.
Our books reveal how each of us participates.
            I am grateful for our collaboration
            and look forward to a mask-free celebration.

Poetry Pauses

Poetry calls us to pause. There is so much we overlook, while the abundance around us continues to shimmer, on its own. Naomi Shihab Nye

During this pandemic lock down I yearn
to glean life outside, not on page or screen.
I want to touch, in-person learn,
to take to heart what I have seen.
        When I pause to reflect and write,
        visions of darkness as well as light.

To glean life outside, not on page or screen,
to take a ride but don't get out of the car,
to drive by forests and farms in spring green.
has been inspiring, renews my spirit so far.
        On pages and screens such suffering hurts.
        I can only take in the news in spurts.

I want to touch, in-person learn.
I want my experiences in 3-D,
talk face to face, feel what I earn.
I want to spark my creativity.
        When I pause to create poetry,
        I want to write what is important to me.

To take to heart what I have seen,
not ignore, but pay attention,
to recreate where I have been.
I want to explore my intention.
        I can deal with uncertainty, unknowing and change
        and know some knowledge is beyond my range.

When I pause to reflect and write,
I know in time I may make revisions.
With age may come some new insights,
bring a change in some past decisions.
        I may never know if what I witness
        may be enlightened or witless.

Visions of darkness   as well as light
lurk in my ever-challenged mind.
Love and hate are ready to fight.
What thoughts will win and bind?
        Poetry explores discoveries and surprises
        throughout some lives, this poet surmises.

April Poem A Day Challenge

Since most days I write a poem,
April PAD Challenge encourages
me to just be sure I stay on task.

I guess April is a month of renewal,
blooming, bursts of color after cold
chilly months. Poetry celebrates.

Trying to express reactions to my
experiences is not always positive.
Poetry opens us up to feel.

I like to think poets all over the world
are concentrating to contribute their
insights and discoveries to share.

There are two days before official April.
Time to prepare with dark chocolate
stash, clean reading glasses.

I want to sit outside in warm, sun to jolt
my chakras and inhale chi. Sometime
in April this should be possible again.

For now I gaze out windows, cocooned
by lock down, eager to fly. The dandelions
and daffodils are yellow beacons.

This April what will poets write about
in these turbulent times? Many float
abstractions about what to do.

This aging crone with less steady hands,
still can pluck computer keys, try to record
these puzzling, disturbing times.

Count Down

In a dream I invent a word game
or more precisely a letter game where
either orally or written, the aim
is to write as many words time permits, share
       both sections, so a counter can count
       how many individual letters to account.

Or more precisely a letter game where
each letter gets a point for a score.
Timers prevent much padding there.
You stop when told and letter no more.
       I'd be a player or timer, not counter as I
       prefer letters to numbers–that's why.

Either orally or written, the aim
is to respond to questions quickly, work fast.
Then transcripts are made–both the same
for counters. Make sure letters last.
       If work on computer, need to print out.
       Clearly the count must have no doubt.

Is to create as many words time permits share
the results the goal of the players?
We need words for letters to transmit
meaning beside a contest for letter displayers,
       Fast focus and fingers are required
       before the time has expired.

Both sections, so counter can count
must be readable and clear
or other players could demand a recount.
The best timing it would appear
       would be segments of seconds or minute—
       enough to get some letters in it.

How many individual letters to account
would be optimal to win?
I'd love to see the letters mount,
but I don't have to participate in
       this count down to victory
       in any answers in any category.

Languishing

Languishing can dull your motivation, and it may be the dominant emotion in 2021. Adam Grant

Even with the COVID vaccine, many people
are not excited about 2021. It was not burnout,
depression, but somewhat joyless and aimless.
They call this sense of stagnation and emptiness—
      languishing.

The pandemic has dragged on.
We develop routines like masks,
hand-scrubbing, social distance,
The acute state of anguish is called
      languishing.

Many are not performing at peak capacity.
You feel drained, despondent and worthless,
cut back work, can't focus, dulls motivation, you
slip into solitude, indifferent to your indifference.
      Languishing.

We name it for a state between depression and flow.
Flow is state of absorption in a meaningful
challenge or momentary bond where your sense
of time, place and self melts away. Flourishing not
      languishing.

Get involved in projects to recapture happiness.
Find new challenges. Try to avoid interruptions.
Give yourself some uninterrupted time.
Daily joy and motivation is a sense of progress. Still
      languishing?

Focus on a small goal. Start with small wins.
A tiny triumph. Stretch skills and heighten resolve.
Carve time to focus on what matters to you.
Choose an interesting project or goal. Stop
      languishing.

Rethink understanding of mental health challenges.
Many struggle despite labels. Give voice to quiet
despair as you light the path out of the void.
Admit when asked how you feel with
      languishing.

My Meandering Mind

Under overcast sky, clouds
bunch for rain, outbreaks
of sun cast brief shadows.

I sit mid-afternoon under the
hazelnut tree. Distracted, I
forget to bring my blue pillow.

My eyes drifted to dandelions'
diminishing yellow blooms.
Clusters of puffballs explode.

President Biden picked a dandelion
for Jill en route to a plane. The press
called it a flower not a weed.

It was a loving, gentle gesture.
She wore a yellow, floral dress.
Both were masked.

Driving home from massage by
the river front, most people on
the streets and in the park,

sat closely together and did not wear
a mask. A dog walker did. One elderly
couple only the woman masked.

Along the highway— homeless, makeshift
shelters and tents. Debris strewn around.
Communities offer different housing options.

Diners dine outside still. We use a drive-thru.
Who is feeding the homeless? The weather
is more pleasant for dining outside.

Schools resume mostly in school teaching
with some bizarre hybrid options. Confusing
for child care and vaccination guidelines.

The apple petals have fallen. The red azaleas
flare. Hummingbirds prefer blueberry bushes.
My mind is as flitty as buttlerfly flights.

After Mowing

Our mower glows after loping dandelions.
He shreds puffballs and strews debris
all over the yawn lawn— too uniform for me.

The lawn has become boring and I sit
amid the destruction in mourning for
living things killed, often before full bloom.

Our wonderful son was mowed down at 19,
by a truck while he biked in Tuscaloosa,
Alabama on a student exchange in 1982.

The bike was for his 19th birthday. He
rode the bus to Tuscaloosa. I was bereft
when he left Oregon for Alabama.

I was devastated when he died, never to
be the same. Grieving hardens a broken heart.
Cracks do not always let light through.

When I sit outside, the dandelions somehow
remind me of Kip. Their glow, feathery petals,
soften heaviness. When they leave, I grieve.

Something about mowing distresses me.
I prefer re-wilding the yard–more wildflowers.
Pruned trees, weeded gardens depress me.

I'd like to sit outside amid straggly grass,
admiring "weeds"–advocate freedom to grow
for all entities. Let lichen, moss, fungus spread.

As I deeply breathe chi and titillate my chakras,
I hope to release pent up sorrow, try to heal.
When it is my time to be mowed down, go

to wherever I may be going–or not, in whatever
form or energy I may or might not be, I hope
I revere light in all its intact manifestations.

Lotus Above Muddy Waters

Our path compels us to rise up like a lotus flower above muddy waters.
Duncan Ryuken Williams

An ancient religious symbol,
with mud indicating suffering,
is important to remember
in these troubling, murky times.

Mud contains the nutrients.
In pure water the lotus will not grow.
We can't distance or transcend trauma,
we must transcend ourselves

Buddhism suggests wisdom times
compassion equal freedom. Wisdom
is seeing things clearly. Compassion
is suffering together, feeling others' difficulties.

Since we are in such an interconnected
time, we cannot avoid the pain in the world.
We must try to repair the negative "isms".
From this muddy base, can we become a lotus flower?

When I see dandelions rooted – sometimes
in mushy ground–I celebrate them. They
are my lotuses. Whatever is happening
around them, before mowed, they bring light.

Without floral inspiration, can we rise up
and accept the challenge to help others?
I feel limited to do so in a pandemic, but
I can praise and protect dandelions.

On this rainy, raw, windy day, rain drips
on my outside chair. I can look out and see
bright dandelions, buttercups, rhododendrons,
azaleas try to lift me up and get me to work.

One Word At A Time

In
a
dream
I
was
hosting
an
event
where
we
were
creating
a
poem
in
a
column
one
word
at
a
time.
Now
awake
I
am
trying
to
write
this
poem
in
this
manner.

It
looks
like
a
jagged
pillar
or
a
loped

limbed
tree–
all
knobby
and
gnarly.

Perhaps
it
could
be
a
dandelion
stalk?
Create
a
concrete
poem
by
cutting
the
words
of
the
column
and
collage
dandelion
blooms
on
top
to
create
a
dandelion
bouquet?

The
dandelion
blooms
could
have
words
on

the
petals.

Maybe
the
words
on
the
petals
could
be
calligraphy
since
typing
in
a
circle
is
not
my
skill.

But
what
could
they
say
about
dandelions
vertically
or
circularly
I
have
not
said
horizontally?
and
should
these
stalks
be
about
dandelions?

Then
what
should
I
do
with
these
columns
if
not
to
support
poetry?

Just
a
nodding
head
exercise
in
prose?

I
doubt
this
idea
catches
on.

Just
a
finger
exercise
on
dark
keys?

Back
to
nap
another
dream
perhaps?

Notable and Famous People

When I made a list of notable and famous
people I have met or seen perform, it was long.
and I am sure I will remember more. These
people have made a memorable impression.

In Corvallis, Oregon
Met: Gary Zukav and Linda Francis
        They came to see their grand-daughter play
        volleyball for OSU. While sitting with a friend
        in a crowded coffee shop a couple asked if they
        could join them. My husband asked them to dinner
        and I almost fainted when he said Gary and Linda
        were coming to dinner. I knew them from Oprah
        and had read several of his books. Court and Gary
        talked environmental issues. We've seen them often.
Jean Auel (Clan of the Cave Bear)at a Calyx fundraiser
        Jean was the featured reader at the event. Calyx took her
        to dinner, my husband paid for hers. Very pleasant.
Saw Perform: Maya Angelou sang and danced at OSU.
        She danced lithely and read poetry with power. Commanding.
Mark Strand: The poet read at the library. Not that memorable.
Taylor Mali—my favorite slam poet reads with an articulate
        delicious, rich voice. I bought a pen which had one of
        his poems scroll out of the side. Very handsome.
John Ashberry: Chain-smoking, obscure poet. Perhaps
        he was drinking as he slurred words.

Haystack Poetry Workshops with
Primus St. John: Young black protégé of William Stafford
        was very nervous and new to teaching. Gentle soul.
Sandra McPherson: She brought her young family. Good teacher.
William Stafford: National and Oregon's Poet Laureate
        hung his poems with students on a bulletin board.
        Low-key, modest, non-directional teacher. I've had
        many workshops with him and enjoyed them all.
David Wagoner: Handsome poet from University of Washington.
        His wife stood at the open door during student critiques.
        To protect him or students? Excellent teacher and could recite
        lines of many poems from memory to make his point. Brilliant.

Richard Hugo: Grossly obese he scratched his crotch lice in class.
    His wife came to visit and we all felt sorry for her. He was
    a good teacher–but distracting.
Lawson Inada: From Ashland where he taught, he was a warm,
    gracious poet but meanders off the topic.

Portland
Met: Erna Gunther: We met the famous anthropologist
    at a reception through a relative. We had seen
    Richard Leakey while grad students in Arizona.
John Nance: The photojournalist came to speak to
    the Children's Book Writers conference about his
    his children's book about the Tasaday. We came
    to know him well and he came to speak at my husband's
    anthropology classes before he moved to the midwest.
    He was very handsome and had modeled. Charismatic,
    and a great storyteller. We met Goody Cable through him.

Saw Perform in Science Series
Stephen Hawking: He rolled on stage in his electric gadgeted
    wheel chair and was in command of his artificial voice.
    He could hold an audience without moving his body.
Alex Filippenko: An amiable astrophysicist. Very engaging.
Brian Greene: Another dynamic astrophysicist. Very articulate
    and clarifying speaker.
Billy Collins: He was an arrogant ass. He tossed questions
    from the audience on the stage as beneath his responding.
    I have not read a poem of his since. Rude and crude.
Alvin Ailey: His troupe are magnificent dancers. I was mezmerized
    by their fluidity and flexibility.
Bob Dylan: We took our grandson to see the aging, gruff singer.
    He was dressed all in white and his raspy voice and solemn
    demeanor did not project a performer, yet intrigued.

Connecticut
Met: Jose Limon: Some of his dancers came to do a workshop
    for the modern dance club at Central Connecticut. We were
    poor to mediocer dancers at best. We must have been a
challenge.
Gary Burghoff (Radar on MASH): Gary had a cottage at the same lake
    in Winsted as my in'laws.. He affected a cane, friendly, but full
    of himself.

Robert Frost at Wesleyan College. We carpooled to hear the famous poet.
He presented himself as the humble rural poet, but afterward
at a frat party, we saw him as a drunk. I stopped reading him.

New York City:
Met: Derek Hough (saw also in Portland). On my 75th birthday I was
visiting relatives. My husband's gift was seeing New York
Spectacular starring Derek Hough still my very favorite
dancer. They said after the show Derek would come out to
greet fans. We formed two lines. He appeared with hair still
wet from his shower, ripped jeans. The woman before me
asked if he remembered her from another show. I chimed in
"How do you expect he'd remember all the fans he meets?"
He said I looked like his grandma and was impressed I had
come from Oregon to see him. Lovely smile and warm.
Gorgeous. My husband took our picture- still framed on wall.

Saw Perform
Martha Graham: In college an aging Martha was still dancing. She
wrapped dark
shroud around her in a grand gesture and unfolded gloriously.
May Swenson: My favorite poet of all read at the NYC Y with William
Stafford. I love her word play and imagination. I was
enthralled. Afterward I saw Bill. He thought I came to see him. I had
seen him many times in Oregon and could not say I did not come to
see him, but enchanting May.

Washington D.C.
Prince: While on sabbatical we took our daughter to see her idol Prince.
He was a scrawny and to me an unimpressive, performer.
Ricky Martin: Also while on sabbatical we took our daughter to see a young
Ricky Martin. He is actually vibrant and fun to watch.
George Winston: My husband is a fan. It was a very enjoyable concert.

I have probably forgotten several other notable and famous
people. I thought as you aged you remembered the past
with enhanced clarity. Not sure that is true with me. Favorite
play-nude Hair in San Francisco and Cats in D.C.

A Chilly, Blustery Mid-Afternoon

Gusty wind makes the backyard
shivery and chases shadows. Sirens,
dog barks, mowers, wind chimes jar.

I carried my blue pillow to soften
my sit and news blaring from screens.
My red cape flaps in the breeze.

A hummingbird nips a blueberry bush.
Several scrub jays peck at bark dust
and the rock wall. Are they opening nuts?

No butterflies. No seen bees. The mower
littered the lawn with yellow floral heads.
Red azaleas and rhododendrons fade.

Lavender and pink petal plants join in decline
as well. White petals dropped. Buttercups
greatly diminished. I miss the colorful spots.

The birds walk the wall near me, look around
and ignore the red-draped statue on a chair.
The sun comes out in intervals, warms my back.

So many headlines to ponder. What can I focus
on? Yard angels Bottom, Airlika and Tootsie
are not enlightened in muted light.

What can I think amid all the concerns and
conundrums facing the world. All the theories
and conspiracies–alternative notions of what's real.

I dwell in lock down illusion and confusion, trying
to get a grip amid uncertainty. How many dimensions
am I living in–unseen or in dreams?

I am a spinning pinwheel, flailing with the winds
of change, motivated into action by my love
of others and the unmet needs of so many.

I go inside to mull and muse in comfort. I wear
the red cape to maintain any warmth I muster.
My eyes feast on thousands of energizing angels.

Writing a Trente-sei

I want to write a trente-sei.
The challenge will be fun.
I'm not sure what I want to say.
The conundrum has begun.
      Will the tone be light or dark?
      Do I muse or just embark?

The challenge will be fun.
The word-play and rhyme schemes
interweave until it's done.
What are my choices of themes?
      During lock down I don't get out much.
      What prompt will be my crutch?

I'm not sure what I want to say.
My inside life limits what I can see.
I rely on screens unfortunately.
I want to be impulsive and free.
      I want to breathe without fear
      and hug close those who are dear.

The conundrum has begun.
Do I explore and engage risk?
I crave warmth of the sun.
Live life as an asterisk?
      Hope that vaccinations
      are at all locations?

Will the tone be light or dark?
Based on reality or hope?
Hit form out of the ball park?
Be a release on how to cope?
      A trente-sei confines
      thought into 36 lines

Do I muse or just embark?
Stay true to form or not?
Invent a form for a spark?
Find a better poetic slot?
      Perhaps I'll just give this form a try,
      stop guessing the reason why.

The White Bird

Sitting under the hazelnut tree
with a clear blue sky and intense
heat above, I move to shade.

Only my legs were in sun. I faced
north. Two scrub jays flew west.
Two white butterflies flew east.

Over my head a white bird flew
to the fence, then into neighbor's
yard. A gray bird followed soon after.

Was the white bird a dove? An albino?
The coos sounded like mourning dove,
but I thought they were brown.

When I went inside I looked up, the symbolism
of a white bird. They express hope for the future
of people and world, good news, peace, purity,

prosperity, peace, honor, noble thoughts, desire
for change, clarity, calmness, love. Pretty impressive
omen. I'd take any or all the meanings.

White irises and white butterflies are regulars—
are part of the yard's allure. After a half-hour power
outage last night, sitting in the dark, only

headlights glow in windows as they pass. The
power company said it could be hours. Today
in warm, natural light, I am grateful for white.

Juneteenth

June 19th we celebrate Juneteenth,
a national holiday. In 1865 Major General
Granger came to Galverston, Texas
with news the enslaved were free-
2 ½ years after Lincoln's Emancipation.
News traveled slowly in the South.

It has taken a long time to become
declared a national celebration. People
will party, parade, create new traditions
with new food. This year our visitors
are from China. No specific celebration,
just a long-awaited visit.

When I sit outside under a cloudless
blue sky, the sun darkens shadows.
One dandelion wallflowers against
the stone wall. More flowers fade and
curl. A scrub jay spreads wings in the
garden. Socially distanced dogs bark.

A Monarch with black-edged wings and
dull yellow and white butterflies flit.
A monarch passes my right shoulder
closely displaying intricate wings.
As my back begins to roast, I contemplate
the flowers. They could be color-coded.

Red roses for Native American, clover
or irises for whites, dandelion or buttercups
for Asians, bark for blacks. Green stalks
and lawns for all who are pro-green.
All plants create a color palette for
our yard and orchard....together.

Juneteenth, like all holidays, we can
celebrate progress in civil rights and
justice for everyone. Some of the Juneteenth
menu does not exactly tickle my palate, but
many foods do not, and I can adapt. In lock
down we needs days to honor freedom.

Graduations

In newspapers and on screens
masked and unmasked graduates
toss their mortar boards outside
before large crowded audiences.

Many celebrations were postponed
last year, so some celebrations had
two classes. In 1958 my high school
graduation had two schools together.

In my senior year the large class was split
to go to two schools. Many stayed at Hall
and others like me to a new school Conard.
Together for three years, we reunited at graduation.

We had to drive into Hartford and Bushnell
auditorium. We had different colored robes.
When we marched on stage, we received a
cover, but the certificate was mailed later.

I graduated from college early and went
to graduate school in Arizona. I did not
return to graduate with my class in Connecticut.
After my masters, my husband and I moved on.

He had his first post PhD job at Carnegie Melon.
We did not graduate with our classes because
we had moved to Pittsburgh. Certificates mailed.
My parents missed post-high school graduations.

Much later I decided to go to the local community
college in graphic design and printing technology.
My parents promised me a typewriter if I went
through graduation ceremonies here is Oregon.

The gown was a purplish-red like a bruise and very
flimsy. Our children wore it as a Halloween costume.
We were lead by bagpipers with kilts. I have moved
on to computers. The typewriter has a broken key.

Now we attend graduations for others. I have degrees
in Elementary Education, Educational Psychology,
Graphic Design and Printing Technology. I taught,
started my own press and have written 12 fantasy

books and over 20 poetry books. Each graduation
opened doors. I still wish I had a degree in English.
I attended Haystack Writing workshops with William
Stafford, David Wagoner, Sandra McPherson,

Primus St. John, Richard Hugo and others and plenty
of Oregon State Poetry Association workshops, PEN
Women and other groups. I host several writing groups.
No more certificates, but made many poet friends.

So as I see mortar boards flying with so many hopes
and unforeseen challenges, I wonder what will these
graduates have to dream and advocate for? I do not
remember feeling daunted, I hope they aren't.

Pillow Talk

Blue pillow to soften black metal
seat under the hazelnut tree and
un-needed Andean hat–no sun

Late -afternoon on a overcast day,
no shadows under the canopies
as I huddle in my jacket from chill.

The wimpy wind barely moves
the wind chimes and pinwheel.
Most blooms have shriveled.

Some small red roses and one
red rose prevail. Center lavender
rhododendron sheds but some resist.

Batches of buttercups and clumps
of clover march toward each other.
A close clover patch has pink centers.

My massage oils me up and loosens
joints, but I am not up for dancing. But
my thoughts race and concern returns.

Conditions open, but what is latest news?
For grieving friends we are a long way
from recovery. We yearn for good news.

Zoom meetings remain. Only Scrabble
is inside and unmasked with vaccinations.
Drive-thru is still eat-out of choice.

In a few weeks we will have been married
for sixty-years. We have postponed a trip
we planned for a year. Life is on-hold.

It begins to sprinkle so I pick up my pillow
which did not soften my mind much–but
sure made it more comfortable to breathe chi.

Poetry Reveals Beauty

The world is complicated. There is darkness and light. Forgiveness comes into view...
To see the world as a poet is to be aware of beauty wherever you go, A poet believes
that beauty is a clue to the essential nature of existence. Jacqueline Suskin

Poetry reveals beauty in the smallest details of creation.
Poetry finds light in the darkest shadow.
Poetry is a teacher, guide, full of imagination.
Poetry explores deep truths joy and pain allow.
     Poetry deals with triumph and grief.
     Poetry brings some healing relief.

Poetry finds light in the darkest shadow.
Sometimes light is very hard to see.
Darkness depresses spirits, stops light flow.
Awe is an alluring possibility.
     I'd like to be light-bearing,
     truthful, resilient and caring.

Poetry is a teacher, guide, full of imagination.
A way to find meaning, ask questions,
use curiosity and seek inspiration.
Poems can offer different suggestions.
     Pay attention to what is around you.
     Discover the uplifts that surround you.

Poetry explores deep truths joy and pain allow.
Some searches rely on agreed "facts".
Most poems aspire to high road, not low.
Poems are poets' persistent creative acts.
     Emotions uncovered and revealed.
     Some left alone and concealed.

Poetry deals with triumph and grief.
Extremes can bring forth intense expressions.
Some poets rely on delusional belief,
some vent with passionate confessions.
     Poetry is an emotional medium.
     Poetry likes sparks, rarely notes tedium.

Poetry brings some healing relief.
Poetry leaks words from your hands.
Readers enjoy poems terse and brief.
Poetry strives for truth and understands
     not all is knowable with constant change.
     Poetry is an never-ending exchange.

Jabber-wonky

What people jabber about is wonky.
Climate change jars normal weather.
Pandemic keeps us from getting together
Political symbols: elephant and donkey.

People who converse with ease
remember names, dates and places,
recall events and everyone's faces
are not jabber-wonkies.

To lose access to memories is understandable
as we age, neurons clog,
connections need a jog,
we have thoughts jabber-wonkable

Sometimes we suppress pain, lose a key
to enter other dimensions, gain access
to what we need for success.
We are behaving jabber-wonkly

I do not feel very wise
in this incarnation, this time
I reflect in poetry and rhyme,
I tend to jabber-wonkerize.

I do not think I am special,
that I have great wisdom to impart.
I just want to play some part
even if I am jabber-wonkial.

I word-play and I hold back going bonkers
in a puzzling, uncertain cosmic dimension
trying to find meaning and intention.
I am one of the jabber-wonkers

I try to observe, comment and not forget
in words what my life reveals.
What my unknowable life conceals.
I am a feminist, progressive Jabber-wonket.

New Words

Merriam-Webster added 520 new words on the
leading language provider website. Some examples
are COVID-19, second gentleman, long-hauler,
flex, AMSR, sapiosexual, but not yeet.

Lexiographers say language changes, and how culture
and social media influence new additions. @ not just
for email, but is also means to respond to, challenge
or disparage the claim or opinion of someone.

Long-hauler now means a person who experience
one or more long-term effects following initial
improvement from a serious illness like COVID-19
which probably most people know the meaning of.

Second gentleman is the husband or male partner
of a vice-president or second in command of a
country or jurisdiction. ASMR is a tingling sensation
starting back of scalp to neck and upper spine.

Flex is informally defined to talk in a boastful or
aggressive way. Sapiosexual refers to romantic
attraction to highly intelligent people. To get in the
dictionary must show established member of language.

Just think there are over 500 words to discover!
It might be fun to write a poem using these newcomers
–perhaps rhyme them? The flex sapiosexual second gentleman
is a long-hauler from COVID-19 and AMSR ...is a start.

The Shadow Knows

There is wisdom when you are no longer afraid of the dark. Sara Wiseman

Shadows of our mind can be scary.
Our wild, reckless, unreasonable, self
unrestrained has much to teach us, wary
you try to suppress, close to protect yourself.
   But opening up can release the muse,
   find other ways for dark thought to use.

Our wild, reckless, unreasonable self
can open creativity, free restraints.
I don't try to be perfect, torture myself.
I've no desire to be among saints.
   I excuse my frailties as humans flaws,
   unbidden and sometimes without cause.

Unrestrained has much to teach us, wary
of information that can challenge preconceptions.
Rethink options to the contrary.
Be prepared for other's reception.
   Darkness contains light like stars.
   Navigate away from what scars.

You try to suppress, close to protect yourself.
What choices can we make to increase enlightenment?
Until life story book is closed and put on the shelf,
did we act with a sense of entitlement?
   Dark situations brought into the light?
   Did we try to uplift humanity's plight?

But opening up can release the muse,
bring fresh expression of one's experience.
Find the spark with the intention to infuse
our inner light, our radiance.
   Put light on any situation
   to allow more penetration?

Find other ways for dark thoughts to use
like increasing awareness, what to avoid.
Learn what dark thoughts to refuse.
A life without light is devoid
   of warmth, kindness, joy, hope.
   Seek the light for ways to cope.

Why Can't We Fly On Our Own?

When people were designed, why
were we not created with wings?
Why are some species grounded, others fly?
What essence is in charge of such things?
       I'm drawn to angels and fairies- a myth?
       Do they actually need wings to fly with?

Were we not created with wings
because we're not evolved enough?
Such freedom having wings brings.
We are all made from stardust stuff.
       We manage to pollute land, sea and air
       The Anthropocene folks are everywhere.

Why are some species grounded, others fly?
Diversity, cooperation, sustainability essential.
I'd love to give my own wings a try.
Think of all the hidden potential.
       We might get internal GPS- not follow roads,
       find many more accessible abodes.

What essence is in charge of such things?
Are we alien galactic transplants? Cosmic clones?
A deity on which religion clings?
Who invented flesh and bones?
       How about wings that are attachable?
       Grow on us and are dispatchable?

I am drawn to fairies and angesl-a myth?
Relying on intuition and unprovable belief?
WIll the truth ever be forthwith?
I could use some aerial relief.
       People are not ethereal beings yet.
       We are different breed —don't forget.

Do they actually need wings to fly with?
We depict them with wings to give them flight?
I concoct them as a word-smith,
not needing proof for these guardians of light.
       In dreams and other dimensions I could fly,
       winged or wingless. They're role models to live by.

Prothalamion for Our 60th Anniversary

A poem in lieu of gifts. We do not need
more clutter. A card or call would be nice
as our family is not in town. A trip later
when COVID passes will suffice.

We have weathered heartbreak and sorrow
as well as happiness, adventure and joy.
We have tried to conquer challenges.
We both have habits that annoy.

We have children, grandchildren, a great grandson.
Many live in Oregon, two—Vermont and New Zealand.
It is hard at this time to connect and to unite.
So much we just do not understand.

We have lived mostly in Corvallis, Oregon.
Connecticut Yankees moved west.
Lived in Washington, Arizona, Woods Hole,
Maryland, Virginia, Connecticut — but Oregon best.

We both published several books.
We both taught–you at OSU and me LBCC.
We traveled the country many times.
We juggled family to get a MS and Ph.D.

We traveled to Sweden several times,
St. Petersburg and Europe to explore,
to meet relatives and see the sights,
we are not as agile anymore.

Lock down can limit the choices we can make,
we still can make memories, take short rides.
We try to help each other, reach our goals,
together see what our future provides.

I still love you after all these years. You are
kind , generous. We are imperfect, yet cope
with whatever life throws at us
and cling onto light and hope.

The Dance

Poetry is a choreography, not a word list–a choreography of feeling, perception and thought. Reginald Dwayne Betts

Words dance down the line
Ideas leap from mind to hand.
Feelings and perceptions flow.
Like any art, can we command?

Birds and butterflies practice routines.
Birds sing a chorus near me.
Butterflies circle, disappear off stage.
Grass waving has its poetry.

I am surrounded by nature's dances.
Even pinwheel joins in when spun.
Flowers pass into summer,
fling petals, in the warm sun.

Human's dance is not as airy,
in costumes which hold the eye.
The variations are endless.
I wish I could give dance a try.

As I watch other dances' variety,
I focus on the movement details.
Toned bodies perform magic.
I know the commitment it entails.

When I was lithe and limber, I tried
many forms of dance.
Now I admire from afar in my
stiff, painful circumstance.

Any form of dance by any species
captures my admiration—
the chance to express their soul
and heart from any situation.

Natural Phenomenon

Deflowering

A new genus and species of flower encased
in amber is about 100 million years old from
Gondwana the ancient supercontinent. It
has unique features not found in modern flowers.

Valviloculus pleristaminis is named from Latin
valva, leaf on a folding door. Loculus means
compartment. Plerus refers to many and staminis
reflects dozens of male sex organs.

Elderly (84) George Poinar Jr. of Oregon State
University probed this ancient flower. Kenneth
Chambers and Fernando Vega assisted with
discovering this new flower only 2 millimeters across.

Some fifty stamens in a spiral arrangement,
anthers pointing to sky and an egg-shaped
hollow floral cup. Six tepals and two chambered
anthers with pollen sacs open with hinged valves.

These ancient flowers cannot be placed in modern
plant families. Scientists have found numerous
angiosperm flowers in Burmese amber. We can
learn more about distant past biology and ecology.

Deflowering in many contexts deprives one
of virginity. With flowers, sexual exchanges
have been going on more eons than humans.
This new flower was well-endowed for the task.

Revisiting the Backyard

For weeks I've been inside.
No sitting outside to huff chi.
The shade is down. It is cold, wet.

The political drama / trauma keeps
my eyes on screens and paper.
I've neglected noticing my backyard.

This morning the shade was up
and an overcast sky matched a gray
squirrel scampering in the garden.

The two hazelnut trees draped seed pods.
Lovely, light branch extensions cascade,
frame Airlika angel dangling from a limb.

The pinwheel is still, as is Tootsie,
the angel weathervane–stuck. Grass
still green with leaf litter skimming on top.

The apple trees are skeletal. I am
content to stay inside on a soft chair,
to watch, for there's no sun to warm me.

Recently, I witness the front yard through
windows. Myrtlewood, holly and camellia trees
are green with red berries and white blooms.

Tiny bluish birds flit between the canopies
as well as a juniper. Our parade of wild
metal and concrete animals shines out front.

I am afraid I ignored the backyard
for front yard attractions. But today's
squirrel and seed pods lure me back.

Sticking Snow

All afternoon the snow fell from
a gray-white sky. Snowflakes
of diverse sizes layered on limbs.

The now-covered leaves cup them
in place. Holly berries sneak peak.
The camellia blooms droop.

The snow did not melt when landing
on the still-green lush grass. Stone
walls grin or grimace.

In the backyard snow drapes branches
cradles the snowflakes. The pinwheel's
blue and white stripes, unfettered and still.

Tootsie, the angel weathervane is stolid.
No snow despite her unwavering stance.
She is gray and blends in with the day.

My thoughts are with the people in line
waiting for a COVID shot. It was cold
earlier, but no snow when we were there.

The shades in office are down to conserve
heat. I peer out un-shuttered windows and
marvel at all the shifts and changes we witness.

Virtual Groundhog Day
February 2, 2021
Punxsutawney, Pennsylvania

Since 1887 a groundhog emerges from
hibernation prompted by instinct
to be greeted by crowds eager to know
if Punxsutawney Phil sees his shadow.

This year the tradition went virtual,
just a few greeters due to the pandemic.
The marmot saw his shadow, so
six more weeks of winter.

15,000 virtual viewers. 150 cardboard
cutouts, some in groundhog gear.
Few media in attendance, just a quiet
pandemic crowd at Gobbler's Knob.

Since a snow storm hit the area,
I am surprised he saw his shadow,
but a beam of sun poked through.
The chilly witnesses had their answer.

I wonder if Phil went back to hibernate
for six weeks more? What does he do
to bide his time? Snow adds to the mix.
Perhaps he is Philomena?

In Connecticut another prognosticator
is named Phoebe. She saw her shadow
at the Lutz Children's Museum in Manchester.
She replaced Chuckles X who died.

Chuck at Staten Island Zoo disagreed
with Phil and Phoebe, predicting an
early spring. Not sure how reliable
groundhogs are as weather predictors.

Groundhog Day is a cross-quarter day
falling approximately midway between
solstices and equinoxes. Groundhog
is first cross-quarter day of 2021.

Members of the Puxsutawney Groundhog
club greeted Phil as he emerged from his
burrow. They were all gussied up in black
with a black top hat, looking very official.

They proclaimed Phil said we are looking
forward to one of the most beautiful
and brightest spring we've ever seen.
Spring 2020 wouldn't be hard to beat.

Phil has predicted longer winters more
than 100 times. Ten years of records lost.
Many years like this, his forecast was in a
major snowstorm. This year is 135th as oracle.

Frontyard Haiku

Robin gulps holly
berry down whole. Yellow beak
holds the berry tight.

What small bird is in
camellia— hummingbird,
bush tit? Anonymous?

Parade of wet wild
animal sculptures strut and shine,
shine in the sunbeams.

In the windows blue
electric candles glow in
the night like starlight.

No sitters on cold rock wall
wall covered with soft green moss.
Few passer-bys now.

Myrtlewood, juniper with
camellia and holly.
Branches flail in gusts.

Regenerating

My waxed amaryllis has two new shoots
after blooming two tall stalks. I wonder
how many times will it up-shoot?

During the pandemic I am creating poems
with less distractions. Generating ideas
from books, screens and observations.

My body is busy generating aches and pains.
My knees still bone on bone. When in a wheelchair
I'm eye level with bellies, tend to look up.

Trying to keep up with changes all around me.
Trying to calm confusion and chaos.
Trying to tame stress and worry.

The regenerative healing of sleep is elusive
with many interruptions to wake me up.
Dreams are surreal, multi-dimensional.

Politics generating division.
Marches promoting love and hate.
Violence in the streets and still wars.

A stabilizing force amid constant change,
peace and unity sought for, mostly in vain.
Dark chocolate my solace, my balm.

Snow Artwork
Espoo, Finland February 7, 2021

Something in the human brain that likes a round form. Janne Pyykko

Artist Janne Pyykko transformed a golf course
into a complex giant pattern in the snow.
11 snowshoe clad volunteers stomped thousands
of footprints for the 525 diameter artwork.

Two days they recreated Pyykko's computer
design into snow and temporary art. A social
challenge to guide and lead the group. A visual
challenge to replica the design on a large scale.

This art looks like a starfish and six snowflakes.
It is the largest snow drawing ever made in
a Nordic country. A snow canvas for art as
well as snow angels, snow people, igloos.

The coordination of measuring and using
assisting strings to construct and maneuver
rounds in cold is impressive. I remember
when I skied, it was freezing. But for art?

Lucky the Finns are not such wimps to bring
beauty to the landscape before gusts of wind
and more snowfall erase their brief art. A thing
of snow beauty is a joy forever captured by camera.

Out the Bedroom Window

When I plan to take a nap,
I am entertained by tiny
blue birds flitting from holly,
camellia, and myrtlewood trees.

The trees block a tall juniper.
Today the leaves shine in sun.
Camellia blooms glow. Wind
shivers the branches.

On weekend drives we see flocks
of black birds performing their
murmurations, plunging into
a green seedy field. But

the blue birds outside my window
are so captivating. I am glad we have
have trees they can enjoy. They
are hints of an upcoming hopeful spring.

The blue birds are up close, fidgety,
eager for flight. They move freely
and take off to wherever they want,
while many people are caged inside.

Observations

Holly and camellia trees
with fidgety, lickety-split birds,
bend branches, glisten in sun

Clear-cuts in forest
do not cast shadows
on the road, wound hearts.

Patches of blue in puffy clouds,
some fringe tinges of gray melding,
cheer rain-watery spirits

Dandelions and daffodils—
yellow caution spots while I'm
over-eager for spring

In lock down for a year
I peer out windows, wait
for warmth to open them

The Dandelion Sentinel

The day after the vernal equinox,
I look through the windows facing
the backyard after rain.

Nuzzled near the stone wall is one
burgeoning dandelion. No mushrooms
or dandelions in the lawn.

The angel sculptures scrubbed clean
by rain and air dried by wind. The trees
still mossy droop over shriveled tan leaves.

My chair and pillow remain inside. Still
too chilly to inhale chi. Sun too intermittent
to rely on for light or warmth,.

I welcome the dandelion in these lock down
times. A Brit friend says he is "shielding."
Glass shields me from the backyard.

I turn inward to inside tasks. Bark dust tamps
garden weeds. I envision a yellow-dotted lawn
and smile at the prospect.

Warming Up

Two days before June, after a massage,
I head to the backyard to warm under
a robin's egg blue sky. Only a few breezes.

I check on the irises, buttercups, fruit
and nut trees as well as swelling azaleas
and rhododendron–all in various stages.

Small green apple nubbins blush when
facing the sun. Too big for birds to gulp,
but growing for larger creatures.

The scrub jays poke around and as I
was getting up–a jay swooshed right
by me, followed by third white butterfly.

Soaked in sunshine, I went inside
for a nap, legs up and lymph flows.
I was in my warm, cosy bed–when

I am startled awake by a voice on a
Zoom call. I am not pleased. I debate
to toss the blanket or hold it tight.

I decide to go to my computer and
warm up my mind and fingers in a poem.
I watch a friend's recorded Zoom reading.

It is time for dark chocolate and to focus.
Like a blurry pinwheel, a rattling wind chime
my mind's at the whim of the windy muse.

Under the Hazelnut Tree

Beneath a cloudless, blue sky
at noon, I carry my blue pillow
to sit under the hazelnut tree.

Beside my chair, a smaller
dandelion sidles next to a larger
one. Relationship unknown.

Apple petals float to the grass
without overlapping each other.
Somehow each petal finds its own spot.

Mid-lawn I see a buttercup–middle-sized
between dandelion and a small yellow
flower near the edge of the rock wall.

Tiny lavender blooms reside with the
small yellow flowers. Dandelions spread
all over the lawn–rarely touching.

Intermittently dogs bark, mowers whirr,
wind gusts rattle the wind chimes
and spin the pinwheel.

A blue jay spreads wings wide to sun
or to dump. Birdsong sporadic. Later
two more jays enter the area.

Joined by a third bird in the pear tree,
they fly west, too close for my comfort.
Rusty angel Airlika sways over my head.

I stop musing over the George Floyd case.
His murder hopefully will bring reform
and justice for all Americans. Dare we hope?

I have been warmed and comforted in my
chair. When I go inside to nap, I have another
respite from the darkness of the world.

The Stripping Tree

Yesterday a hacking crew attacked
the tall redwood across the street,
strewing branches over two yards.

At one point a worker screamed
three times in acute pain before
he either passed out or exited area.

My view through the front window of
the stripping tree is obscured by my scruffy
holly, camellia and myrtle wood trees.

But today the Christmas tree at the top
of the lopped off limbs is gone. A ladder
leans against the knobby trunk.

The ground debris still strewn across
the lawns. It is mid day and the crew has
not returned to remove the tree remains.

I bet they return with their sawing and jawing
when I want to take a nap. My shade is open.
Why did they take down such a towering tree?

I will miss seeing it when driving home
or from my window. It is painful to see
branches stripped, trunk with warts.

Sunny-side Up in the Backyard

At 4, I carry my blue pillow and iced tea
to jiggle chakras and inhale chi
under angel Airlika on the hazelnut tree.

My chair faces east, back to the sun
my neck and back baking has begun.
It is 82, long sleeve shirt has won.

Apple blossom petals, open white
from pinkish buds, freckles in sight.
Slivers of apple chips in flight.

From a rhododendron a blue jay drops,
follows fence under azaleas and stops
to peck bark dust from earth for bird crops.

The blue jay has hues darker blue than sky.
White belly impractical? I wonder why
white prevailed? Gave black a try?

The jay flies to the fence post, does a survey,
flies to neighbor's backyard to foray.
Why does the bird have to fly away?

Hours earlier the hand mower loped the lawn.
Dandelions and clover became a pawn,
leaving butch cut grass a level-headed yawn.

Barking and traffic murmurs in the distance.
Locally wind chimes sing in wind resistance.
Pinwheel spins at wind-gusts' insistence.

Several white butterflies fly over the grass.
Some flights rather close, do a by-pass,
fly to neighbors' yards alas.

A discordant bird call from neighbor's yard,
sounds abrasive, harsh and hard,
urges me to leave–a cronish diehard.

Backyard Flights

Bees nuzzle apple blossoms,
shake petals into free fall.
Petals white-spot the lawn.

Tall, white-headed puffballs
blanche from gray, toss
seeds with the breeze.

Low-lying dandelions escape
mower. Too tall puffballs annoy
the hand-mower also.

Numerous white butterflies dart
in all directions. Few land in transit
to other yards. Fewer bugs today.

One deep orange butterfly with
black-edged wings hovers near grass
and the rock wall before flying away.

Two blue jays land on the peach tree.
They greet beak to beak and depart
in opposite directions. One lingers

before visiting fence, power lines–
climbing to top line before choosing
where to go next. Solo again.

One blue jay has gray near head
and high back. Elderly bird, or a special
species spread wings in the bark dust.

Another jay soloist prefers pecking a nut
on a rock, exiting into the rhododendron.
But soon a crow caws from neighbor's tree.

The sequences vary 1-6 caws. Some sound
urgent. Several guttural growls do not
lure company. Caws seem in vain.

A blue jay briefly perches on a lower limb,
but does not respond to the crow, leaves
crow in the lurch on his lonely perch.

My mind flies free to interpret meanings,
just observe, take my own flights of fancy.
Thin clouds gauze sunny, blue sky.

Dandelion Profusion

Front yard
dandelion dots
burst yellow rays, splat
in batches in the lush spring grass,
glowing.

Nearby
camellia
limb pecked full of holes, hosts
red-headed woodpecker in
same spot.

Drilling
for insects or
worms? Lots of tree to go!
Dandelions entice bees before
puffballs.

Robins
and bluebirds seem
to prefer the holly
berries, to bounce on branches so
gently.

Below
dandelions watch
near larger taller blooms.
Daffodils trumpet yellow and
bring spring.

Shine

Sun shines on glistening holly tree.
Sun shines on other trees, but
no leaves sparkle like holly leaves.

Sun shines on the cars' tail lights
lined in the clinic parking lot.
Those lights not facing sun are duller.

Sun shines on noses above the masks.
The colorful designs enhance many faces.
We have been having sunny, chilly, spring days.

On the days with less or no sun, I miss shine.
The shine on metals, on any surfaces
that shine back from sun.

On the days with less or no sun, I miss shine,
look for daffodils and dandelions to remind
me of renewal, things opening up.

On the days with less or no sun, I miss shine.
Before lock down we took shine as an expected
treat. When the gloomy days come, I yearn for shine.

Watching A New Bird

Over the years the holly tree
expands and gets closer to
the front window.

I am used to seeing bluebirds
and robins stopping by to rest
and to gulp the red berries.

But a new bird: black head
and back, rust -colored wings,
white belly seems to stare at me.

The window frame becomes
a large tv—more vibrant than
the TV beside the window.

I get binoculars to see if my
aged eyed really spot dots
on this bird's back.

Of course, then the bird faces
me and I cannot see the back.
The new bird, I cannot identify, leaves.

A red-headed woodpecker and
hummingbirds seem to prefer
the tree I think is a camellia.

The white petals have dropped,
but the holly berries remain. The
woodpecker pecks one spot on trunk.

At least these birds do not crash
into the window following an illusion.
I'll watch, social distanced, unmasked.

Inside birdwatching is a pandemic pursuit.
Outside I am lured by daffodils. As spring
approaches, I look forward to sitting outside,

to survey the backyard and observe changes.
I wonder if the birds can see me and if they
even bother to look, content among branches.

Under Uncertain Skies

The gray/white clouds play tug of war
with blue sky. Shadows come and go
with intermittent sun. Wind gusts
jangle wind chimes and whirl pinwheel.

I sit on my blue pillow under the hazelnut
tree, gaze at yard angels, azalea blooms,
watch a few bees and birds, listen to
several bird calls in a distance.

My red cape repels the chill. Then
a large blue jay swoops and snatches
a small gray bird poking in the bark dust.
Away the jay flew with the bird in its claws.

I was stunned and pulled my hat strap
under my chin in case jays like hats.
Why would a jay attack another bird?
When I went inside I researched jays.

Blue jays are members of the Crow family
and are vicious carnivores. They eat mice,
bats, fish and other small song birds. They
eat 3 times more plant matter than meat.

I loved jays' birdsongs and gorgeous blue
coloring. I never dreamed they preyed
on smaller birds and ate them. I am so
disappointed and will view them differently.

Sometimes I see two jays together on a branch
but mostly they fly alone. They sit on the highest
power line and scout. Before they seemed just
interested in plants, perhaps some insects.

I wish when this planet was seeded, there was
a way to nourish all creatures without killing.
How about pills with only non-conscious ingredients?
What if everything has consciousness? What then?

Overcast

At noon in the backyard, the overcast
sky displays only momentary sun to warm
my red cape, lighten my spirits.

I sit as if a red light under the hazelnut
tree. Not enough wind to spur wind chimes
and pinwheel into motion. No butterflies.

Birds chirp in other yards, fly above my head.
Perhaps I broadcast grumpy vibes. Bees in
blueberry bushes. Red azaleas popping.

Since yesterday a dozen puffballs emerged.
Younger yellow dandelions disperse slowly.
We protect the bees with no sprayed blooms.

A friend's son died. I have been there. I
tear up with grief. It is appropriate no sun
shines–just sunbursts of comfort.

Discordant cacophony of caws, do not
sound like birdsong. A lone blue jay's
raucous call seeks company.

A gray squirrel scampers on the top
of the weather-worn, wooden fence –
so frisky and bushy-tailed.

Tonight's April full moon is called
the Pink Moon. I will look up and
try to inspirit some light in darkness.

Puffballs

Balmy, calm day with wispy
cloud tails. When I sit under
the hazelnut tree— its curvy
shadow touches the angular
roof shadow. Puffball seeds float.

Somehow I've become a puff magnet.
White seeds enclosed in a dust ball
type fluff float from growing puffballs
in the lawn and garden. They do not
fall directly to ground, but waft.

Puffball seeds park on my shoe,
surround the chair, place precisely
near me. Only two were touching
in their descent and stay connected
in the grass and nuzzle.

Several barely miss my arms
and legs, cuddle close to me.
The tiny white seeds have found
their special spot to grow. Yellow
dandelions enjoy their place in sun.

Butterflies flit, but rarely land. Blue jays
dump in their garden spot dot landings.
Pinwheels and wind chimes whir and whine.
But the silent yellow and gray sentinels
catch my welcoming eyes first.

Sun-Baking

At noon under denim-blue sky
which matches my jeans and
white clouds which match my hair,

I carry my blue pillow to sit under
the hazelnut tree and sun-bake in
my long-sleeved shirt, covered with words.

Dogs em-bark on a lengthy conversation.
A train whistles in the distance.
Wind-chimes and pinwheel move gently.

A fly visits a dandelion and a bee buzzes
my body. Some puffballs appear moth
bitten before they puff fluff stuff.

White butterflies fly seemingly rudderless.
Hummingbirds bother blueberry bushes.
A blue jay perches on the roof.

I am an island in a green sea absorbing
sun. An ant crawls blade to blade. My neck
muscle is sore from misplaced pillow.

The chitter-chirps of birds is constant companion.
I listen without understanding, unlike Ted Cruz
who snoozed through Biden's speech.

Azaleas flame beside the fence. Red spitfires
in the rhododendron. Most white petals blown
from trees meld into the lawn. Branches begin fruit.

When I feel saturated with sun, calm my mind,
reflect on the daily changes I see in my domain,
I carry gear inside to the shade, artificial light.

On Beltane

Mid-afternoon on Beltane, under
a blue sky with fragmented clouds,
bird shadows fly overhead.

I sit out of shade with the underbelly
of metal angel Airlika overhead and cement
angel Bottom on a blue table beside me.

Tootsie, the weathervane angel remains
stuck in northwest. Breeze tickles wind chimes
and twirls the pinwheel like a wheel of fortune.

White butterflies blend with white blooms,
apple blossoms gone. Bees are basking
in the warm sun, just as I am.

Strawberries begin flowering white, a Beltane
symbol of first fruits to ripen in spring to bring
luck, romance, sensuality and fertility.

The check list for Beltane begins. I am
spending time in nature admiring one
dandelion and buttercup the mower missed.

The Fisker hand-mower left tall stalks,
bent over blades, uneven grass, but loped
many dandelions, puffballs, small flowers.

Hummingbirds prefer blueberry bushes, but with
blue birds visit lavender and red rhododendrons
and red azaleas huddled near the fence.

I wish I could shake my booty and dance.
We support climate change and environmental
causes, we tend our lawns and gardens.

I am meditating on the forces of life and spring
as I evade shadows and lean toward sun. I can
celebrate mildly, yearning to be flagrantly wild.

Noisy Neighbors

Conversations of neighbors
on both sides of the fence,
waft into the yard where I sit.

The loud words carry in the sunny
75 degrees mid-afternoon air.
I can tell what they are discussing.

Birdsong from hummingbirds in blueberry
bushes, blue jay squawks, dog barks,
irritating wind chimes surround me.

White butterflies silently fly by on their
jagged flights. Lady bugs in the grass.
One buttercups, two dandelions- silent sentinels.

Numerous gray-headed puffballs, occasionally
shed fluff. Azaleas and rhododendron emblazon
with blooms along the fence. I resonate with noise.

As much as I like quiet, I love color and movement.
A friend asks how I avoid being depressed by world
event. I admit I am down, but words and sounds refresh.

As long as I can carry my blue pillow
into the backyard to commune with yard angels
and nature, I feel uplifted, can carry on.

When one neighbor starts
using the hose to fill a plastic
pool, I've had enough and go in.

The Magical Flower

When I move my backyard chair for sun,
nearer to the round, blue table holding
prone cement angel Bottom, I park
near a tall puffball. I pick it and blow.

I study the tiny white seeds wafting
gracefully into the grass. Such fine
filaments shining in the sun. I beat
the mower to free these seedy tufts.

Puffballs have a parachute system unlike any
other found in nature–four times as efficient
as modern parachute designs. Scientists
can apply to engineering sustainable technology.

So dandelions are magical–not a troublesome
wide-spreading weed, but a wondrous
ingenious, beautiful flower I cherish and
want them to flourish in our backyard.

Bottom, hosts a black fly who seems
to fancy the hard, curly locks of hair.
The fly also has a brief respite on
the table before taking flight.

My husband stops after a bike ride to loll
in the grass. Soon he pops up and starts
pulling tall blades sticking up in the garden,
out the rock wall or towering over grass.

I ask how many dandelions he sees.
He reports two and yanks the tall blade
hindering the spin of the pinwheel. A
Gust sends the pinwheel reeling.

The wind chimes catch wind. Neighbor
children shout hurray in several cheers.
Tootsie, the weathervane angel, does not
budge and stays tooting northwest.

Our son told me about dandelions, these
delightful dandelion puffballs with a parachute
system better than our own, which is why I stare
at the puffball so intently and smile at seeds' flight.

A Manipulated May Extended Sonnet

Mid-afternoon on a sunny May day,
a few filmy clouds scuttle away.
A dull brown bird collides with the pinwheel.
Wing and blade clash. Both safe from reel.

A spiderling thread hangs from the peach tree.
When caught by the sun, splotches are shiny.
One dandelion remains, buttercups muster,
about two dozen blooms for a bouquet cluster.

The white butterflies and bees are sparse, maybe
don't find azaleas and rhododendrons tasty?
Puffballs have lost their floral appeal.
Perhaps the birds' choices are not ideal?

Birds chirp in a noisy filibuster.
They are a tranquil mood buster.
Maybe they hope I'd go away,
so they can continue to sing and play.

I focus on the scraggly grass at my feet.
Ants climb their blades. My sonnet is complete.

Baking as I Bask

Under thin, striated clouds,
sitting in the sun surrounded
by shadows, I bake.

A hat protects my face, but
the rest of me is ready for
roasting. The warmth soothes.

The mower left no puffballs,
two dandelions and two buttercups
in the still uneven lawn.

White butterfly which might be
cabbage moths are usually solo.
But two circled each other in greeting.

They converse but briefly before
continuing their own flyways. Two
bluebirds did not land.

A hummingbird pecked blueberry
bushes. Apple blossoms are gone.
No white petals in the grass.

I absorb the warmth and try
to wrangle diverse dark thoughts.
When my back feels hot, I leave.

Inside I pluck black keys with blue
letters–like the sky–at night and day.
I am glad blue is on top.

Count down in Lock down

Day after day the floral count
fluctuates in the backyard.
Today down to one puffball
and seven buttercups.

White blossoms scarce. Some
small flowers in the strawberry
patch amid tall blades of weeds.

Hummingbirds and bluebirds
and some brown birds enjoy
the trees and bushes. Hummingbirds
nuzzle blueberry bushes.

Bluebirds poke around the azaleas
and rhododendrons. White butterflies
swerve in diverse directions as if drunk.
Spider threads shine in sunbeams.

Lovely blue sky and warm sun
bathes me in calm and beauty.
As I count the changes each day,
it is like pop-up art in my own gallery.

After such a balmy stretch, I have
to prepare setting up places inside
and outside for three sets of visitors
tomorrow, in case it clouds over.

Visitors are rare these days so
I want to be a good host and
have favorite foods on the menus.
My husband will cook–lucky for them.

Tomorrow will be a special day when
I will have a break from sitting alone
in the backyard on my soft blue pillow.
I can interact with friends and family.

Breaking Free

Mid-afternoon Sunday, the family gardener
drags a long hose across the back lawn
to sprinkle a young blueberry bush.

Half of the hose is black and half green,
attached together for the long-haul.
It slithers like a snake on steroids.

I sit near the west hazelnut tree beside
a radiating dandelion. Only a few puffballs
with few dandelions seeding.

Two hordes of buttercups approach
toward the yard's center. If they march on,
the backyard could be polka-dotted with yellow.

Metal angel Airlika hanging on a west hazelnut
branch shines with sun on her head, horn
and upper torso– so luminous.

Bluebirds land on the peach tree's skimpy
pecking branches. Few leaves again this
year. We hope for two or three peaches.

The white butterflies' uncertain, neurotic flights
keep me guessing where they'll land. They
have their own GPS it seems.

Birds uplift my spirits as they fly freely,
unaware of the grounded beings,
still stuck in lock down.

Blue birds peck in bark dust and tree limbs.
Butterflies like strawberry patches as white petals
are gone from apple and blueberry sites.

As the sun rays pelt my back, I am reluctant
to leave. Sunburn and nose cancer risks prod
me up from the chair. I carry my blue pillow inside.

I am grateful for the wind chimes and pinwheel
who stir my thoughts— the winged and floral ones
who share their brief residences in our yard.

Indoors amid the inanimate world it is awhile until
I feel I have my wide-brimmed hat on. I am flying
with my imagination–no need for hats or boundaries.

A Windy, Early Afternoon

A Scrub jay lands spreads wings to poop.
The green hose tangles loop over loop,
sprinkles for the garden to regroup
travels through a buttercup troupe.

The buttercups march to the center of yard.
Flanks moving west and south across backyard.
No bees or butterflies pester or guard
against this persistent floral boulevard.

Puffballs blow their precious wad,
dispersing a dandelion squad.
Our mower does not applaud,
but I want dandelions to laud

The wind is a tad chilly.
The bumpy lawn seems hilly.
Wind chimes and pinwheel move willy-nilly.
Deep breathing chi and shaking chakra's—silly?

Metal angel Airlike hanging in hazelnut tree,
toots her horn west away from me.
Shaded, she is dully shiny.
Tootsie, weathervane angel faces west permanently.

Dogs bark meekly next door.
I don't want to hear more.
I want my spirits to soar.
I hope for no lock down anymore.

A mourning dove coos.
How does it affect my blues
after reading and seeing the news?
Does one have the chance to choose?

A contrail scars blue sky, appear
with gathering clouds, hasten to clear,
then a sprinkle of rain falls near.
I want to head out of here.

Then with a silent adieu,
my sitting time is through.
I have other things to do,
just the same as you.

The Concert

A cacophony of caws, coos, chirps
and squawks continued constantly,
hidden in canopies, flying in profusion

as I watched through windows. Rain
came and went. Wind gusted and quieted.
I have never seen so many birds in our yard.

They appeared agitated and did not
land in the yard or garden in my sight.
The constant chatter unnerved me.

Only two met briefly on the power line.
The rest were on solo flights. They invade
the two holly trees in the front yard.

The backyard buzzed in constant turmoil.
The blue table holding angel Bottom became
speckled in raindrops and pelted him.

The buttercups' two flanks advance toward
each other. Yard angels Airlika and Tootsie–
the calm amid the swarm, the pinwheel, a tilt a whirl.

No dogs bark, no butterflies seen, but wind
chimes tune in. Something was stirring activity
with or without the stimulus of rain.

It is too wet and windy to sit outside.
My sock-feet touch slate. My red cape
repels the chill. I am puzzled by the commotion.

Distracted from darker thoughts, I go inside to ponder
them. Later I peek at a breezy backyard. Scrub jays,
mourning doves probably other birds still croon

Looking for Kaleidoscopes

A group of butterflies is called a kaleidoscope.
Sitting outside I saw only solo one.
Any other ones were beyond my scope.
My scouting for them has just begun.
      My fritillaries like to clique.
      These butterflies exit – quick.

Sitting outside I saw only a solo one—
never landing—just a flyby.
White wings shine with sun.
Dandelions do not even try
      to fight the mower.
      I praise dandelion power.

Any other ones were beyond my scope—
lost in azaleas or rhododendron bushes?
I want to see a flurry. I continue to hope.
Butterflies social distance as a scrub jay swooshes?
      Birds in the orchard, ant army in the grass.
      Buttercups march into mower's morass.

My scouting for them has just begun.
Inside thousands of angels kalaidoscope everywhere,
not in a tube, but color spread, collecting undone.
These inanimate wings keep me aware
      of winged ones in many creations
      and many ways for animation.

My fritillaries don't like to clique
like my host of angels who maybe sing together
on a different wave length they can pick
without concern for the weather.
      But in my backyard I must sit and wait.
      Butterflies continue to hesitate.

These butterflies exit— quick
to other gardens in other yards
with a zig-zag route and a wing-flick.
They go with my best wishes and regards.
      I am grateful they lighten my day
      and don't want mowers to keep them away.

Calm Between Storms

After morning showers, I
go outside to sit and ponder,
under cloud-crowded sky.

No birds appear, except
overhead, until a goldfinch sat
on the sparsely- leafed peach tree.

Then a brown-speckled bird,
much larger than the goldfinch,
pecked at the wall moss.

No white butterflies, but buttercups
begin their after-mowing revival and
proliferate rapidly. Dandelions stall.

Irises are late-bloomers to the garden. White
petals droop like tongues, from a pallid plant
flower named for the Greek Rainbow Goddess.

It is chilly, luckily not windy. Pinwheel
and wind chimes get respites. Distant
traffic murmurs. Few dog barks. Birdsongs.

When the sun rays bring brief shadows
and I am about to warm–bam— it's overcast.
I hug my red cape, re-drape my knees.

I try to evoke joyful thoughts and happy news.
In my local, peaceful bubble, I need to heed
bubbles elsewhere are breaking.

Rain sprinkles the backyard. I bid farewell
to the yard angels, greet inside angels.
Now at my computer, my words take flight.

For the Record

Mid-afternoon under cloud-fuzz
on a blue blanket sky, I sit under
the hazelnut tree, out of shade.

Only one scrub jay found an open
spot in the garden to belly flop,
spread wings to sun or exit waste.

When finished resting and a stomach
scratch, the scrub jay flew away,
ignoring a nosy white butterfly near by.

Ten white butterflies scope the area.
Two duos circle each other and fly
in different directions–Butterfly Express?

No evidence of dandelions, but fluff floats
around me. One seed with transparent wings
and an orange, duck beak lands on my leg.

The east flank of buttercups assembles
a battalion marching toward the west flank,
slowly to recruit and is pretty stagnant.

The white irises let it all hang out. Each day
more blooms open. The rhododendrons are
surrounded by a petal pond beneath.

The azaleas shed faded petals. Birds pick
between bark dust and fallen petals. Wind
and air mild. Sun on angel's backs, Bottom's belly.

Only a few woofs from neighbor's dog. A few
birdsongs, traffic muted. It is a quiet, peaceful
retreat today. My back warms without a jacket.

A neighbor starts to water his lawn. I figure
it must be about time to go inside. I've warmed
my body, breathed deeply, adjusted my chi.

The Red Butterfly

In the backyard I have seen monarchs,
yellow and white unmarked wings, and
today my first red-winged butterfly.

At first I thought the wings might be
a deep orange-red. But as it flounced
around me and kind of leap-frogged in grass,

I could see the wings were red with a
few markings. Just one among white and
yellow counterparts. Flying art.

When I went inside, I looked up the meaning
of seeing a red butterfly: an important message
is on your way. Some had positive or negative

beliefs, depending on different cultures. I hope
I see more red butterflies whether message
or warning. In these uncertain times,

lots of deception, lying, fear. I will concentrate
on beauty and hope–welcome red butterflies
to our pesticide-free backyard.

Before the Mowing

At one the sun is out,
I dash outside to sit
under the hazelnut tree
to stir chakahs and breathe chi.

All day clouds billow and move
on. While it is sunny, and before
mowing later, I try to get some sun.
I wore borrowed sunglasses.

The sunglasses make the colors
more intense. Green is lusher.
Soon, the backyard was about to get
mowed. Yard and flowers leveled.

The clover and buttercups expand
their patches. The clover has four
and the buttercups has two batches.
They could wind-wave in the grass.

They march across the lawn, two
floral brigades intertwine at the edges.
Irises, azaleas, rhodies wither and
drop petals to ruffle the bark dust.

The red roses remain vibrant. A monarch
swings near me, multiple white butterflies
make solo flights across the yard. No
mourning doves. Just a little bird-chat.

For a little while, the world feels less
heavy. My back and knees warm. The
wind and temperature fluctuate with
cloud coverage. I hug my jacket tight.

When it starts to sprinkle, I decide
to go inside even if I did not get a full dose.
The mower guillotines the taller flowers,
lops white and yellow heads, levels lawn.

At least before the mower, I see individuality
in the flowers and blades. I like the scraggly
look. Some tall ones bow and escape the mower
to pop up. The small will inherit the yard–briefly.

Negotiations

On an overcast early afternoon,
I venture into the backyard with my
blue pillow and Andean hat for an
uncomfortable sit. Jacket zipped.

Gusts of wind wiggle the buttercups
and tall clover. The pinwheel shifts
directions in spinning confusion. Loud
wind chimes jangle my nerves.

Just as I decide to go inside, the sun
bursts through the thick gray clouds.
I told the sun as soon as clouds appear
I am going back inside.

I can deal with wind gusts animating
the floral and arboreal life forces.
Petals fall. Irises sway. But no sun?
Why go outside and be cold?

As my back warms, I settle in.
If my turbulent thoughts would
disappear, I could relax. I urge
them to let go, but they stayed.

Then the clouds returned. I saw no
benefit, as light shadows left. Yard
angels did not shine or move. I pick
up my pillow to moodle inside–warm.

Circling Butterflies

While sitting in the backyard, butterflies
on their erratic flights survey the garden
and sometimes land. Brief visitors.

Sometimes two butterflies come from
opposite directions, circle each other
without touching in a circle dance.

I read they flutter, synchronize, circle,
spin, form knot patterns and spread
unseen chemicals and pheromones,

which drew them together. After they
circle, they fly away again in different
directions. Beautiful dancers.

Butterfly wings' are intricate designs,
flying flowers, color swatches in air.
Some drest and climb grass blades near me.

I study them when I can and do not
disturb them. I could be a weird tree
or statue to these agile art palettes.

One landed on my knee. I did not move. I
rudely stared and welcomed the butterfly. I
remained silent. I wish I could dance with them.

Let Us Entertain You

As soon as I sit down
beneath the hazelnut tree.
A red-headed hummingbird
flies beside me.

It spotted a bug caught
in a spider's string.
A shiny red headdress
and wings fluttering.

Next on stage is a duet dance
by butterflies connecting, most solo.
I am glad they have company,
then alone away they go.

The petals have fallen, browned
on the ground. Only the roses remain.
The yard is a green spread.
Red roses poke into view again.

Irises, azaleas, rhododendrons shrivel.
Bugs crawl and balance on a grass blade.
Clover spreads like mayonnaise.
The buttercups march on parade.

Wind chimes sing with gusts of wind.
Pinwheel spins in hot air.
A dog barks when neighbor chats.
Cloudless sky everywhere.

A place of solitude amid turbulence.
The show today warms my heart.
I go inside carrying my pillow.
I'm eager for tomorrow's show to start.

Some Like It Hot

Yesterday we reached 107.
Portland set a high of 109.
Today at 10:30 it is 95 here
and could climb much higher.

I sit in the shade of the hazelnut
tree. Sun peeks between the leaves.
I am patchy with light. I have my hat
and comfy blue pillow.

Not much evidence of floral or
winged life. Our neighbor's lush
backyard would attract more
bees, birds and butterflies.

One yellow butterfly in our yard
and one yellow butterfly flits in
their yard. Two scrub jays grub
blueberry and rhododendron bushes.

Cloudless blue sky, little breeze.
Wind chimes, angels, pinwheel
bask in the sunny stillness. Only
the murmur of route 99 traffic.

Forecasters say coastal winds will
cool the valley and stir things up a bit.
But I've done my outside bit and will
cocoon inside–away from pandemic.

My husband biked before 8 and I sat
before noon. My afternoon sits postponed
for awhile. I like it warm, but not too hot.
I'm getting to be a fussy old crone.

Backyard Delights

Butterflies flutter
to stalk, leaf or bloom, zig-zag
over garden and lawn.

White butterflies tend
to loop, unpredictable
flight patterns, amuse.

Monarchs' black-etched wings
open beside me, mostly
solo. White ones dance

Dual dance circles
join from distance, then they part
to different spots.

Jays on power line,
bark dust, branches, grass, stone wall
fence— glimmer sunshine.

Hummingbirds flicker,
fast-winged dippers, slow brown birds
less energetic.

Gust-driven wind chimes
accompany bird songs, barks.
Our pinwheel whirls.

Bees in white clover.
Three tall dandelions light-sparks.
Buttercups— lawn-stars.

Every day there are
small changes, details noticed.
Uneven grass bends.

As I sit, angels
are nearby, vigilant while
I chuff chi, deep-breathe.

The Red-Leaf Clover

I'm looking over a red-left clover
that I overlooked before. Clover
and buttercups struggle over which
will cover more of the lawn.

Fruit matures blobs on the
branch. Apples tinge pink,
pears— not golden, peaches and
plums hide behind leaves.

Tall, dandelions tower over
the grass, wave in the wind.
Most flowers withered. Fourth
of July in two days. Yard explodes.

Fireworks are illegal in much of
the state. Fewer pets spooked.
Some patriotic events will take
place, social distanced.

Our Everyone Can Join parade
seems to be a go, but I am not
sure I will go after years of loving
this eccentric parade.

Tomorrow an outside poetry reading
in Salem. An indoor lunch is legal.
Oregon is one of the low-COVID rate,
as a high percent are vaccinated

Emerging from a massage, a yellow
butterfly flutters around me in a chaotic
pattern. We have butterflies in our yard,
but the birds give us a pass-over.

When I sit outside, each day the scene
makes small changes and sun winks
behind hazelnut leaves, speckling my skin
until the sun musters enough heat to burn.

The mutant red-leaf clover is one of a kind
for me. I am careful not to step on it. Too low
for the mower? Tall dandelions sprawl, gain
more sentinels to survey their domain, like me.

National Focus

A Dark Day
    January 6, 2021

As a stunned nation and world watched,
Trump ignited a mob to attack Congress
to impede the vote to certify Biden/Harris
electoral votes to win the election.

Protesters who believe Trump's lies
and delusional fantasies overpowered
barriers and security to enter congressional
chambers planning to take hostages.

Armed, mostly mask-less marauders
carrying Confederate battle flags, stealing,
entering offices of members of Congress,
were intent on hanging some adversaries.

Four were killed in the attempt. One woman
shot and three from medical emergencies
on the day COVID took the most lives
in one day in our nation. National guard called.

Some members of Congress with escape hoods
evacuated, some retreated to their barricaded
offices, some flattened to the floor until all
chambers were cleared by police.

Eventually they reconvened and after some
objections to the validity of the vote in some
states, Pence droned on to finally certify
the electoral college votes for Biden/Harris.

When they adjourned it was almost 4
in the morning. Talk of Trump's sedition.
Talk of more than 52 arrests and responsibility.
Talk of 25th amendment and impeachment.

Trump says he is the best first term President,
while most call him the worst. He conceded
Biden won and there would be an orderly
transition amid reports he is insane and incompetent.

He desecrated the Capitol, encouraged a coup,
threatened democracy, embarrassed us once again
in front of the world. With only 13 days left he is still
a threat and dangerous. His social media cut off.

We wait to address pressing problems and to hold
accountable those who endanger our lives. It
is an appalling event, a disgrace, shame and stain
on our democracy and flawed leadership.

The next day Pelosi said if 25th amendment is
not invoked, impeachment proceedings should
begin. For the sake of the country I hope they
remove him, before he inflicts more damage.

His disastrous presidency has caused harm
in so many areas-environment, education,
justice etc. Now isolated, he still has codes
to nuclear bombs causing fear around the world.

Fallout

In the aftermath of the siege on Congress,
many issues have been exposed.
Many accountabilities we need to address.
Many penalties to be imposed.
    We all must be diligent about our facts.
    This is the price our freedom exacts.

Many issues have been exposed.
Too many hate groups in our nation.
Many questions need to be posed,
requiring a truthful explanation—
    police conduct, racial injustice,
    inadequate protections for all of us.

Many accountabilities we need to address.
So many questions and ways of prevention.
So many charges on perpetrators to press.
Who will take charge of this intervention?
    Red-hat fanatics formed this mob.
    Police did not do their job.

Many penalties to be imposed
on the leadership and domestic terrorists.
Many methods have been proposed.
Still the injustice, hate, fantasy persists.
    They have begun arresting some participants,
    identified on Internet by lawful inhabitants.

We all must be diligent about our facts.
Fake news, lies, alternate reality
effect some folks, provoke angry acts.
Many lost touch with actuality.
    We must avoid being duped and maligned.
    For love and light most people are aligned.

This is the price our freedom exacts.
We can peacefully protest, but not destroy.
Some looters stole national artifacts.
These methods we must not employ.
    Dig deeper for the truth. Be responsible for good.
    Act wisely. Uplift the nation's and world's mood.

Seeking Redemption

Many people urge us to think
Of the positive from congressional coup
which lead democracy to the brink.
I am not feeling gratitude–are you?
        Domestic terrorists threatened our nation.
        Everyone demands an explanation.

Of the positive from congressional coup,
young pages carried and protected electoral votes.
Some members of Congress–too few
switched to support Biden–this sugarcoats
            their involvement in four years of lies.
            Other deluded folk support Trump tries.

Which lead democracy to the brink?
Inadequate security? Failure to discover plot?
All this makes our heart and mind sink.
This mob casts a stain and a blot.
            Belatedly, they begin to make arrests.
            Different from Black Lives Matter protests.

I am not feeling gratitude–are you?
Perhaps the upheaval will address changes
needed in society as we seek what's true.
Many discussions and exchanges
            need to happen to make progress
            and bring about international success.

Domestic terrorists threatened our nation
under the direction of our president.
Many want to act fast, with his termination.
Less than two weeks left as White House resident.
            He must be held accountable and not hold office.
            Impeachment or censure, 25th amendment suffice?

Everyone demands an explanation
no matter which viewpoint one might hold.
We wait with mounting frustration
for forceful leadership that's bold.
            What do we say to disappointed allies,
            children— to all this act applies.

Briefs

Mad
Donald,
defeated,
refuses to
leave.

Pence
Don's pup
barks back to
break the tether,
rein.

Stop
the steal
by stopping
electoral count.
Bah!

Mob
climbs mall
to attack the
Congress members'
lives.

Trump
incites
violence,
a deluded
mob.

They
threatened
to kill, maim
Congress members–
hang.

They
commit
sedition.
Democracy
pales.

Bring
in the
Capitol
cops, National
Guard.

Was
it an
inside job?
Republicans
helped?

Buzz
on a
vicious plot,
conspiracy,
coup.

Our
nation
embarrassed,
world-wide, frightened,
sad.

Our
Congress
ill-prepared
with security
plans.

So
far we
stopped the mob,
democracy
lives.

Martin Luther King Jr. Federal Holiday

We may all have come on different ships, but we are in the same boat now.
Dr. Martin Luther King Jr.

A pause before Biden's inauguration,
A pause before Trump's impeachment.
A pause to vet security troops.

All these rumblings about other sieges.
All these rumblings about conspiracies.
All these rumblings about COVID casualties.

It is a time of uncertainty.
It is a time of lax leadership.
It is a time to sieve out the truth.

Martin Luther King Jr. broadcast injustice and inequities
Martin Luther King Jr. spoke truth to and for power.
Martin Luther King's Jr. message carried by Black Lives Matter.

We need a pause in all the stress.
All these rumblings generate fear.
It is a time for moral reckoning.
Martin Luther King Jr. had some good ideas.

Stunned

A second Trump impeachment is just.
Senate must complete the process.
Keep him from office is a must.
Sedition charges need to make progress.
 Hope is dimmed across the land—
 very hard to understand.

Senate must complete the process.
They will not issue other choices.
But for justice to be a success,
we must listen to muffled voices.
 The mob show humanity at its worst.
 We must restore democracy first.

Keep him from office is a must.
The liar is an embarrassment.
We need a leader we can trust.
We have had enough of his harassment.
 Despicable Donald is mentally ill,
 He can cause damage for days still.

Sedition charges need to make progress.
It may occur when he's out of office.
He incited a mob to attack Congress.
What punishment would suffice?
 I am stunned and shocked this happened.
 Time for freedom and democracy to remain opened.

Hope is dimmed across the land.
Our past is not as great as they suggest.
Too much white supremacy in command,
causing upheaval, oppression and unrest.
 We need to find redemption,
 not a free pass exemption.

Very hard to understand,
we are such poor learners.
Some think we are grand,
others are flag-burners.
 Divided we fall, united we progress,
 but not with poor leadership and fake press.

Biden/Harris Inauguration

Snow flakes stopped.
Sun came out. Blue sky.
The oaths were taken.

Biden on one Bible.
Harris on two.
Bibles held by spouses.

Social distanced chairs
in audience, but platform
crowded. Three ex-presidents.

Biden becomes the oldest president.
Harris is the first woman and
mixed race vice president.

Everyone was happy, relieved
the event went without a hitch.
Lady Gaga sang the anthem.

Garth Brooks and Jennifer Lopez
also sang. Amanda Gorman,
the first youth poet laureate shined.

Truth, diversity and unity were themes—
preserving democracy, decency and civility
after a seditious siege was a commitment.

Obama, Bush and Clinton with
wives went to Arlington with newly
elected leaders. All appeared congenial.

Tasteful dressed in American and
minority designers–purple was a trend.
Melania left with overseas designer' clothes.

The Celebrating America show was shown
without ads and featured essential workers
selected for achievements as well as celebrities.

I sat hours before the TV witnessing the return
of hope, strides toward inclusion, role models.
After four disastrous years, we need relief.

We have COVID, un-doing damage,
re-engaging alliances, tearing down
walls, climate change addressed.

Biden signed many executive orders.
Harris swore in three new legislators.
On the job right away. So refreshing.

The leaders had to walk for long distances
and stand for long periods. Jill Biden
had spiky heels. She carried on.

It was a sunny day here as well.
May the light filter through darkness
and bring on positive change.

Bernie Sanders Memes

Hatless during the Biden / Harris inauguration,
Bernie bundles up with mittens and a brown
parka. Unruly hair flew in the wind.

Bernie's mittens were recycled wool made
by a Vermont school teacher Jen Ellis
who has a side business, now a mitten frenzy.

His parka on his website sold out several times.
Bernie is dedicated to make sure working people
in Vermont and across the nation get relief

Bernie does not come across as a fashion icon,
but Burton Snowboards' winter jacket sparked
many memes. Go Bernie.

The old man sat with arms and legs crossed
buffeted by this outfit, creating some commerce.
He raised 1.8 million for charity.

They even offer a crocheted Bernie doll
in this garb. Meals on Wheels, aging agencies,
primary care dental centers— a few who benefit.

I was a supporter of Bernie early on. I wear
a colorful, artistic Bernie tee shirt, short-sleeved
so convenient for shots, like first Covid shot.

When I get my second, I will wear it again.
His distinctive hairdo and voice draw attention
even if not as a provoker of memes.

Celebrating Betty Friedan
February 4, 2021

Betty Friedan founder of NOW-
National Organization of Women
wrote The Feminine Mystique in 1963.

She supposedly started the second
wave of feminism discussing women's
"problem that has no name".

Women who did not want to be
limited to the domestic sphere or
lose their identity were unhappy.

Women who wanted more than
role of housewife-mother were accused
of "penis envy" and neurotic.

Many laws and cultural expectations
were made by men. Antagonists proclaimed
feminism was anti-family, anti-men..

Careerists, not overbearing mothers, were
accused of raising maladjusted children.
Some women wanted children and careers.

Well-educated, mostly white middle class
women were the target. The movement expanded
to all women and started a cultural shift.

The Civil Rights Act of 1964 prohibits discrimination
based on sex, race, color, nationality and religion.
NOW ended ads' segregation by gender.

NOW is an intersectional feminist movement that
addresses under-resourced populations: Black,
Indigenous, People of Color and LBTQIA groups.

My mother gave up a teaching career to be a
housewife and mother. When I was determined to get
a Masters and teach, she called me "too competitive".

When I read The Feminine Mystique I felt validated
and motivated to pursue my dreams. I was a wife,
mother, but I wanted to be a teacher and writer also.

I joined the editorial board of a feminist press
Calyx for over 30 supporting a diverse group
of women writers and artists.

I raised three children and returned to teaching
creative writing, children's literature and life
story at a community college.

After I retired I focused on my own writing–
over 20 poetry books and 12 fantasy novels
with my own press Rainbow Communications.

I was determined not to live through my children's
lives and successes. I made my own mistakes
and grew as much as I could with my perceived vision.

My husband and I are NOW members and we have
marched in Women's Marches and for progressive
causes sparked by Betty Friedan. Thank you, Betty.

Mardi Gras Floats

All around New Orleans thousands of houses
are being decorated as floats because
the coronavirus outbreak canceled elaborate
parades mobbed by crowds during the Carnival
season leading to Fat Tuesday.

Trying to find alternatives, pandemic replacements
as scavenger hunts for trinkets usually thrown
from floats and street cars as well as outdoor
art and drive-thru or virtual parades.

Megan Joy Beaudreax suggested people turn
their homes into a float and toss beads from
the attic at neighbor's passing by. Subgroups
evolved to discuss neighborhood plans.

They request houses be decorated two weeks
before Fat Tuesday with addresses with the hope
gawkers will spread out widely in time and space.
They are starting their own Mardi Gras krews.

Some hire krews who make the floats and buy
out of work Carnival artists' art. Spread sheets
of artists and vendors appeared. Crowd funded
lotteries raised funds to put krews to work.

Virtual parades are new pandemic perks. Many
people can see parades in the comfort of their
homes. They can mask up, social distance,
throw beads, join the festivities. Float on.

Yardi Gras

Things turn out for the best for those who make the best of the way things turn out. Jeanne Phillips

Since 1857 Mardi Gras has been called off
14 times due to war, mob violence, labor disputes.
This year was 15th, no parades due to the pandemic.

The skilled artists who create the floats
turned over 3000 houses in New Orleans
into "house floats", thus Yardi Gras.

Gawkers can walk or drive by.
Gaudy, garish, beautiful sites.
The artists were employed.

On-line you can see the flamboyant
flowers, colorful animals and people,
even signs among the wonderful designs.

Maybe not as many floats as the days
of parades, but hopefully recorded
for downloads for years to come.

Idled floats could be seen in city park.
Bars closed. Small gatherings encouraged.
The pre-Lenten bash had a novel resurrection.

The celebrations continue inside
and outside the homes. Creativity
saves the holiday. I rattle my beads,

deck my neck with them in the confines
of my home with leftover blue lights in
the windows and around the front door.

Dealing with Absurdities

Anyone who can believe absurdities can make you commit atrocities. Voltaire

I don't take credit or blame ancestors
for any achievements or flaws.
I'm responsible for my own beliefs and settling scores,
not for in-laws or outlaws.
> Absurdities surrounds us.
> Investigation can ground us.

For any achievements or flaws,
part of the human experience,
I try to curl in my claws,
and exhibit some intelligence.
> Am I my brothers' or sisters' keeper?
> Beyond surface I must dig deeper.

I'm responsible for my own beliefs and settling scores.
To sift through absurdities is my job.
Fake news, mis-information, rotten cores
lure people into a violent mob.
> Peacefully protest for what one finds to be true?
> Be sure authentic facts are behind what you do?

Not for in-laws or outlaws,
but for the betterment of all people.
I try to advocate for a life-enhancing cause,
not swayed by government or steeple.
> Action or inaction may be required.
> Act only when I feel inspired?

Absurdities surround us.
Continual Trump's hubris and lies.
Governments are in a ruckus.
People fume and fuss.
> Uncertainty, poor leadership causes pain.
> I hope we never elect a Trump again.

Investigation can ground us.
Second impeachment is underway.
Absurdities confound us.
We must restore democracy some day.
> I'm tired of processing the absurd.
> I hope common sense can be heard.

The 55th Super Bowl

I didn't want to watch the game.
I wanted to see Amanda Gorman read.
I didn't know either team's name.
They did have a female referee indeed.
    But I missed the poetry reading–too late.
    It was half-time and the Weekend wasn't great.

I wanted to see Amanda Gorman read.
The first woman to read at a super bowl.
A beautiful, gifted black woman planted a seed
for more diversity and culture not grunt and growl.
    She highlighted essential workers in original poem.
    She made the occasion her own.

I didn't know either team's name.
I'd heard of Tom Brady, but not his team.
He's old for a player's time frame,
but played for another MVP dream.
    The ads are not as good as touted.
    Unfortunately, the Chiefs were routed.

They did have a female referee indeed.
Her long blonde hair blew in the breeze.
She was masked and up to speed.
She carried herself with poise and ease.
    I hope females don't want to play with males
    with all the violence and brutality it entails.

But I missed the poetry reading–too late.
She read in pre-game festivities it appears.
I'm so glad she could participate.
Football is not exciting to me. Field clears.
    Stadium filled with confetti as audience leaves.
    Impact as important as one believes.

It was half-time and the Weekend was not great.
A hodgepodge of weird costumes, smoke, light.
Bandaged faces, synchronized marching, fan bait.
Fireworks, glitz, disjointed choreography, bright
    blinding shine amid the Covid ban.
    I'm not a football or Weekend fan.

Winter Advisories

15 million people in 25 states
faced winter advisories on
Valentine's Day and today.

Today in Oregon it is sunny, but
cold. Power being restored, limbs
on vehicles, roofs and roads removed.

China and UAE spacecrafts orbiting
Mars and sending photos from
15,000 miles away.

Pandemic still requires masks,
hand washing, social distancing.
The advisories this winter are harsh.

Corvallis is a nugget of calm
with power and light limbs damage.
No snow and less rain than elsewhere.

The nation is muffled and muffed
in masks and mittens, very cold.
To be warm and powered is lucky.

I sit at the computer with outside
wind chimes jangling near the window.
Shades drawn to keep out the cold.

Later I will emerge for a B-12 shot,
soak in sun and be grateful that family
is safe from scary sojourns to the coast.

Double Whammy Lock Downs

2021 is starting a little rocky.
First lock down for COVID, then
a severe winter storm keeps
us inside. Sometimes without
power for days, encased in snow,
ice, wind-gusts, dropping branches.

Masked travelers face added alerts.
Slick roads blocked. Cleanup
has started as temperature drops,
ground cover melts. Today is sunny.
Things appear to be looking up.
I check on friends and family.

Political instability after Capitol raid.
Ball-less Republicans refuse to
impeach Trump. What does he have
to do to be held responsible for his
actions and threats to democracy?
Everything feels uncertain.

Corvallis was in a "sweet spot"–no snow,
fewer limbs blown down. We have
power. Oregon never looked so beautiful
to me–lush, green, my beloved Enclave.
Oregonians are creative and mostly sane.
Wind chimes outside by window make me smile.

A Wintry Day
    February 19, 2021

Driving home from a massage
on a chilly afternoon, I saw
a bundled up person on the
sidewalk either sleeping or dead.

This person endured a hail storm
during my massage, unprotected
beside a downtown building. Few
people walked about.

Would an officer or social worker
find this person and bring him/her
to shelter? Some tiny homes are
being built, but tents line roads.

Tents mushroom in parks. We have
seen a significant rise in homelessness
since the pandemic. Some tents cluster,
but most are isolated, alone.

Much of the country is in lock down
due to COVID, icy, snowy, frigid
conditions, bursting pipes and flooding,
overloading the power grid.

Defenseless people escape the safety
net. We were not prepared for a extreme
weather or a pandemic. Many have been
left out of the cold.

Academic Disruption

Now as many students learn
by Zoom on-line, separated
from peers, I recall my
splintered schooling.

In our town in the late 1950's
we experienced a population
boom. New schools we built.
Students shifts a needed.

My husband attended four
schools up to middle school.
My shifts waited until high school.
I attended three schools in high school.

One was an experimental program
for gifted students which separated
me from the school I was supposed to
attend and would attend one year.

I was in the first graduating class
of the new high school which separated
students again. A core of girlfriends
met after school and weekends.

We had slumber parties and did
not worry about illness. The students
today have months more on-line,
in lock down and quarantined.

The adjustments I had to make were
nothing to what my grandchildren and
great-grandchildren could face. Fortunately
my grandchildren are in their twenties.

But my unborn great-grandson faces
such a divisive, challenging future.
Until I have had a second shot I can't
hold him for several weeks after that.

So many mothers forced to work
from home, home school their children,
lose jobs, suffer from storms without
power–even to work on computers.

This is when at 80 less mobile and in lock down,
my thoughts are with the families ill-equipped
for such challenges. I have endured and witnessed
other trials. We'll see what we can survive now.

Storms

Storms bring winds, rains, snow
to the Willamette Valley. Branches
land on roofs and cars.

Portland and Salem harder hit
than other places. Power is down.
Snow snarls many areas.

We are in lock down, the instigator
of the storming of Congress
has been acquitted.

But in Corvallis the rain has stopped.
No snow and some sun peeks through.
Much of the nation embroiled in squalls.

But when I heard of the acquittal,
my heart sank for the nation. No
shining light at Capitol Hill.

Women's History Month

Why do women need a special month when
they are half of all global experience?
We don't have a special men's herstory month, then
all genders equal? When everyone's intelligence
        brings respect and self-control,
        opens options for assigned role.

They are half of all global experience.
Women deserve opportunities, freedom
from oppression. When will people uses some sense?
When will divisions and diversity be welcome?
        Suppressive cultures lose talents and gifts.
        What are the mechanisms for uplifts?

We do not have a special men's herstory month, when
they receive special recognition. They have
upper hand in laws, macho beliefs, do not open
access for women, or know how to behave
        when women are empowered,
        or their bloom de-flowered.

All genders equal? When everyone's intelligence
is put to work, new perspectives and solutions
so all can receive just recompense
will lead to more fair resolutions?
        I am losing hope and trust
        changes will be made as they must?

Bring more respect and self-control
to everyone. Persist and resist.
Toss false beliefs and rigamarole.
It is time for women to insist
        boundaries be broken,
        no one is a token.

Open options for assigned role.
Throw out limitations, expectations.
Everyone is healing to be whole?
Develop more healthy, relations?
        Time to rise up and shout.
        Time to let higher self out.

Hunting Season for Geezers

All these old men preying on young women.
What makes them think these women want them?
Pathetic pleaders and controlling men,
trying to get under women's hem.
  Can't they control their lust?
  For the sake of decency, they must.

What makes them think these women want them,
unless these women expect to increase their power.
Why not hold out for a younger gem?
What happens when things go sour?
  Perhaps they exploit each other?
  I don't understand why they bother.

Pathetic pleaders and controlling men
have very little reciprocity to offer.
Male privilege, cultural sexist acumen
compensate with perhaps their coffer?
  Why would women want a decrepit dud
  when they can romp with an virile stud?

Trying to get under women's hem,
makes many women prefer to wear pants.
Less easy access— ahem?
Reduces assaults perchance?
  Women are not safe in many places.
  Trafficking rampant for all races.

Can't they control their lust?
Think with their brain not penis?
Until men and women can build trust
a gender gap remains between us.
  Women are not a slab of meat
  or an after dinner treat.

For the sake of decency they must
act with kindness, respect and love.
Women can demand equity, not disgust.
Women should not expect respite from above
  Stand tall women, you are life creators.
  Don't kneel to male deflators.

The Masked Ones

At the eye doctor's office waiting room,
I look at the masks-such diversity,
not one the same. I don't get out much
but when I do—I enjoy colorful masks.

The boring blue surgical type masks
and some antiseptic white ones,
can't compete with the more fashionable
folks. Many faces are probably improved.

Think of the acne, sunspots, wrinkles
concealed. Some add face shields.
The dental staff had mask and shield
combos. Some masks are doubled.

Then I read Texas and Mississippi
opened up and masks not required.
The newscasters called them "Neanderthals".
Are they loosening restrictions too early?

We may be wearing masks for a long while
yet, even after most are vaccinated. Of course,
anti-maskers let their face hang out and
expose their ignorance, misguided actions.

When we go out we are asked to mask,
social distance and hand wash. Some
schools are opening, hopefully with
vaccinated staff required. Children masked.

Perhaps a bank robber or evil-doer will be
identified by their mask? All these eager eyes
waiting for change. All the deaths, all the
confinements. Someday we'll warm our faces again,

with scarves instead of masks. Someday our
glasses will not fog. Someday we can breathe
freely and just worry about halitosis. Someday
we can embrace hope not fear. Someday.

Headlines Poems

We're breaking through the bubble...Planning to fly? Set your expectations.
New York Times headlines for headline poems.

Reverse Pattern

We're getting our COVID shots, masking, social distancing,
breaking through lock down restrictions little by little
through adherence to safe, suggestions
the doctors are advocating to stop the spread
Bubble we hope we can burst.

Planning to gather in larger groups
to see people face to face, not on Zoom?
Fly? We do not escape masks on flights.

Set your goals for now and future dreams.
Your isolation can bring insight, reflection.
Expectations can lead to greater creativity.

Suggested Pattern

During this COVID pandemic we're
struggling to adapt, intent on breaking
restrictions, following guidance to break-through
the isolation, lack of groupings and contact, the
factors keeping us in our own bubble.

New conditions require new planning
to cope with changes, to
allow our spirits, souls to fly.

Our new intentions may not be solidly set.
Lots of uncertainties, searching for your
core beliefs could challenge expectations.

Brain Buzz

My mind swirls in its bony cage.
Thoughts buzz–some sting like bees.
Pain radiates from all the outrage.
Never experienced times like these.
         In lock down time to recollect,
         examine, pause to reflect.

Thoughts buzz–some sting like bees.
The global news is alarming.
I'd like some good news –please.
The responses are disarming.
         I'll watch bees in dandelions and clover
         until the pandemic spread is over.

Pain radiates from all the outrage
of shootings, climate change, unsustainability.
Fear leaps from screen and page,
overwhelming our capability.
         Isolated, adapting to being in lock down,
         trying to smile, upturn the frown.

Never experienced times like these—
even in wars, then some community support.
Mask, social distance, puts one at ease?
Only dire news and sadness to report.
         Many people are depressed.
         Many feel dispossessed.

In lock down time to recollect.
Uncertainty makes things fuzzy,
anxiety makes me introspect,
keeps my overloaded brain buzzy.
         I have little control in the situation
         and what's humanity's destination.

Examine, pause to reflect,
try to act on what you can?
What pathways can I select?
Will I be a liberating partisan?
         Bees are endangered by pesticides.
         People are also in peril, taking sides.

First Zoom Funeral

Having the funeral on Zoom
for someone who had extensive
family and friends on both coasts
was a wonderful idea.

Those who could not attend could
participate and support the mourners.
A Rabbi said Kaddish for Mourners
in Hebrew and English via Zoom.

The text was on share screen.
The background was muzzled
behind some speakers at the funeral.
Crying infants, tearful adults hugged.

No images of the deceased man of 44.
He was beloved by many for his wit,
brilliant intelligence, and kindness.
He left no children, but good work.

Our son died at 19. First I was in shock,
numb, then agony of grief. I still miss him
and tear up. When my friend returns,
I will know her heartbreak and break mine again.

It was pre-Zoom when our son died
in 1982, beloved, childless, athletic prowess,
filled with light. I am grateful for the time
he was with us, but mourn what was not to be.

Through a psychic I learned he was not to live
long when he came in to redo childhood. He
is sorry he hurt me so, but thanked me for letting
him fulfill what he came back briefly to do.

Every time someone dies young, I wonder
what the cosmic plan was and if there are
no accidents, only exit points predetermined
before you are born in your life chant.

Whatever is our destiny, those we leave behind
mourn. To love is to risk loss. The more beloved,
the deeper the pain. Some wounds scar deeply
within. Sometimes healing feels impossible.

Moodling on Mother's Day

Due to the pandemic we could not
gather the family to celebrate Mother's
Day for all mothers in the family.

Mid-afternoon I sat outside under
overcast skies. Neighbors on both sides
were outside. One mechanically mowing.

I spoke with the gardening neighbors
socially distanced with a fence and
I was mid-yard under the hazelnut tree.

Their son is the age of our younger son's son.
Our oldest son who died young is a bittersweet
memory on Mother's Day and always.

I observe the buttercups are expanding.
Two dandelions and numerous puffballs
ready to seed a new generation.

There is a puffball in the strawberries.
Birds dismayed by mower noise? Even
the wind chimes seem wimpy. Pinwheel still.

When the backyard calms, I can focus on
my mother and other family mothers. I feel
grief for the losses, put my head in hands.

Being a mother has brought joy and pain.
I've been a mother most of my life. One
day of commemoration for birthing life?

Celebrate the women who chose not
to be mothers and contribute in another
way? Some women do both–juggling.

Each woman has her ideas about motherhood.
Some had no choice to be one–no control
over their own bodies and suffering.

Every day should be Respect Life Day
for all species in whatever form they express
themselves. Care for their earthy home.

Remembering What is Lost

The day before Memorial Day, midday,
I sit under the hazelnut tree to remember
all the family and friends I've lost.

I recall special moments and imagine
if we had more time together, what
they could have become, why they left.

Ants crawl in the grass. A white moth leaps
on my right calf of my pants. I gently urge it off.
One monarch butterfly flies over my shoulder.

A white butterfly flies beside me about a foot
away. Butterflies zig-zag in all directions. One
duo does the circle dance in air and part.

The scrub jays zip in all directions as well–
aerial and grounded. They hop along walls, peck
open ground, spread their wings on bark dust.

Much of these routines repeat, just like mine.
We share the same domain. I watch them,
they ignore me. They must know I won't swat them.

The buttercups continue their advance toward
contact. White clover also in the lawn are about
to be mowed—head whacked, uniformly shellacked.

I recall images of when they flourished, like beloveds
I have lost. After the hurt and pain dims, I am left
with my memories–which fade like cascading flowers.

Memorial Day 2021

The battle for survival wages
in the backyard. The mower left
one puffball by the compost heap.

Decapitated buttercups strewn
in chopped grass. A few tall stalks
somehow bent to escape the blades.

This morning the mower massacred
the lawn. Inside I meet with my collaborator
on formatting and illustrating Angels Encore.

She photographed sections of my over
3000 angel collection for ideas on wings,
gowns, my preferences. 12:34 we finished.

The backyard was leveled when I went
outside. Already the sun was warm,
smudges of thin clouds allowed shadows.

The garden attracted several scrub jays
and white butterflies. Both winged-ones
perform circle dances, but don't touch.

When the scrub jays spread wings
in bark dust, I have theories, but not
proof what they are doing–solo.

The irises just continue to grow and thrive.
Red flowers fade. Lavender blooms shed
petals, but many do hold on. Birds hide in them.

The gardener who is also the mower, sets up
the sprinkler to water the strawberry patches.
More tiny nuggets in the apple tree.

This backyard war is humans against nature.
Humans nourish and kill. I prefer to sit in
a wily, weedy garden, not slaughter field.

I prefer to think of peaceful things, living
loved ones. I wish them a happy day, carry
my pillow inside, balanced by my walker.

Residues After Mowing

The day after mowing, the lawn litter
contains floral beheadings and diminished
buttercup and clover clusters.

Some stalwart stalks escape the blades,
wave with the wind over defeated companions.
With strong gusts the new wind chimes ring.

A monarch and white butterfly circle each
other then fly off without touching. Several
white butterflies flit in and out of the yard.

It is about one. Scrub jays poke in the bark
dust and spread wings in the dump spot.
One jay stayed so long I was afraid it was dead.

One jay perched on the weathervane angel's
head, but Tootsie held her position. Airlika angel
in the hazelnut tree speckles with shade.

A neighbor in her backyard chats with
her grand-daughter. No bird chirps. No
dog barks. My back bakes in the sun.

In the wider world Biden and Putin made
some progress. Heat threatens black outs
in Texas. Mortar boards toss all over the country.

I look at the remaining wily grass and laugh
at their resilience. I welcome their resistance
and enjoy whatever diversity is left.

Global Events

Massive Darkness

Trying to maintain truth and light
amid the darkness of lies, sedition,
climate change, COVID, upheavals
can be a daunting task.

When darkness swirls around, how
do you remain balanced, clear-eyed,
as vision is deceived or portrayed
on screens with violence and pain?

How do we hold responsible those
who destabilize with acts of omission
and commission? The zealot faces
of rage and delusion frighten.

Justice is slow to arrest and identify
those who attack government buildings.
States brace for the extreme fringes
to terrorize locally. We pay for the damage.

Has the world become too inequitable
and delusional? Are people seeking escape
and want to blame others for their uncertainty?
Can they find a deeper truth within?

Many are tired of being cooped up with
COVID, unemployment, lack of access
to a vaccine. Frustration leads to misguided
actions and anger to rage. We need light.

World Caring Day

What if we had a World Caring Day
to express love, kindness and gratitude?
What if we acted in a sharing way
with a positive upbeat attitude?
Perhaps we could heal planet and everyone
in need of support, bring back the sun.

To express love, kindness and gratitude
we could donate time, resources, actions
for rebuilding, appreciating and include
diversity, truth and productive interactions.
A phone call, email, letter is a start–
any gesture as way to take part.

What if we acted in a sharing way
to encourage participation and unity?
Many efforts are underway
helping to ensure continuity.
People want warmth and peace.
People desire a stress release.

With a positive upbeat attitude
each of us can find ways to give
and helpful discoveries to intrude,
restore, invent, pursue, forgive.
If all the world found common ground,
perhaps a new normal will be found.

Perhaps we could heal the planet and everyone
with global intent and resolve.
Can the destruction be undone?
Can hate and inequities dissolve?
With many modes of communication,
can we reach every nation?

In need of support, bring back the sun
to warm, grow, push darkness into shadow.
Beam light. A revolution has begun.
This is what World Caring day would allow.
With momentum we can't stop it.
What celebration could top it?

International Holocaust Day

January 27th was chosen to commemorate
6 million Jews and 11 million others
killed by Nazis who chose to eliminate
many of their non-Aryan sisters and brothers.
>   Today the pandemic kills millions as well.
>   We remember the holocaust as deaths swell.

6 million Jews and 11 million others
killed in gas chambers in concentration camps.
The toll on future breathing smothers.
Lost contributions as hate amps.
>   Think of the children never to grow.
>   What they could accomplish we won't know.

Killed by Nazis who chose to eliminate
certain groups for their affiliation.
An extreme way to discriminate
and cause the collapse of a nation.
>   The skeletal corpses, human stack piles,
>   haunted gazes of doomed exiles.

Many of their non-Aryan sisters and brothers
rounded up into cattle cars, stars on chest.
While the world watches and not bothers
to act quick enough and do their best.
>   Some countries will not let survivors enter,
>   with policies that are a preventer.

Today the pandemic kills million as well.
Poorer nations will not get enough vaccine.
Richer nations don't have enough to quell
their own outbreaks on their scene.
>   Global cooperation is a must.
>   We need leadership we can trust.

We remember the holocaust as deaths swell.
Masked, social distance, clean hands,
hope for vaccine, cooped up where we dwell.
We follow as decency and health demands.
>   Horrid memories this Holocaust Day
>   with horrible issues unconquered today.

Chinese New Year
Gong xi fa cai February 12, 2021

Today starts the year of the Ox.
The celebrations signal the start of spring.
The date changes each year as does
the signature animal.

During the 15 days of Chinese New Year
people decorate, give gifts, hold family meals
with traditional food, light incense, clean
their homes and dress in new clothes.

Fireworks at midnight, dragon and lion dances
drive away evil as they pray for good luck.
Evil spirits do not like red, so they dress
in red and bright-colored clothing.

They give "lucky money" in red envelopes.
Businesses close for a week. Many return
to work on day 8. The pandemic limits large
gatherings and they must social distance in restaurants.

The Chinese New Year is for family gatherings,
a time for farmers to relax and pray for next
year's harvest. We have left the year of the rat.
The year of the ox is more appealing.

Since we are expecting a great-grandson
in February I find the attributes of an Ox baby
are diligence, hard work, determination, strong,
reliable, fair, conscientious, calm, patient,

honest, methodical, inspiring confidence
in others, trustworthy. Lucky colors: white,
yellow, green. Quite a positive birthright.
I greet him with love, hope and positive vibes.

Creators of Multiverses

As of February 1st 2021 there are 4414 planets in 3257 systems. 722
systems have more than one planet.

The cabal, council or committee creators of the universe—
they planted entities in the vastness of space.
Diverse dimensions, designs and densities in the multiverse.
Earth received 3D problematic human race.
It is incredulous we are alone
on this planet we claim our own.

They planted entities in the vastness of space.
Each incarnation an experiment?
Each manifestation in the right place?
They let us puzzle what consciousness meant?
Befuddled Earthlings called them divine.
But how would they choose to define?

Diverse dimensions, designs and densities in the multiverse
may have progressed at a different rate.
They could have myriad forms, some better or worse.
The Magnitude of possibilities are hard to contemplate.
Goals may be different for each congregation.
Results differ at each destination?

Earth received 3D problematic human race.
Many hope to achieve 5D vibration.
Then we could evolve at a higher pace.
Would we be in an elevated situation?
Did I land here seeded from the Pleiades?
Did I select conditions like these?

It is incredulous we are alone.
Telescopes spot possible Earth-like planets.
But beings adapted to another place prone
to their own realms not just exo-planets?
Some may be in vaporous clouds.
Or to us frigid or hot shrouds.

On this planet we call our own,
are we exploiters or stewards?
Dealing with climate we can't postpone
or extinction is where we're heading towards.
We don't have the means to populate stars.
Too many people to go to the Moon or Mars.

Who Knows What is Going On?

"Do you ever wake up in the night and just think I'm full of hot gas? "David Letterman asked Rush Limbaugh. " I am the servant of humanity. I am in the relentless pursuit of truth. I actually sit back and think that I'm just so fortunate to have this opportunity to tell the people what's really going on?"

Does anyone comprehend what is going on
spiritually, scientifically, politically, culturally or
do we just cling to an illusion, divisive belief upon
which, when we fog our brain, can we still take a stand for?
> Which approaches can end oppression?
> Which approaches lead to progression.

Spiritually, scientifically, politically, culturally or
with poor leadership, gurus, organizations to guide us,
we do not seem to have learned from what was before.
How long can a suffering planet abide us?
> Climate change, violence, stretches our tether.
> Do we have solution to bind us together?

Do we just cling to an illusion, divisive belief upon
which we determine the path to our destination?
We must weigh evidence, experiences pro or con.
The life on this planet faces extermination.
> Do we have the will or means to make changes
> to bring us into sustainable ranges?

Which, when we fog our brain, can we still take a stand for?
What are reliable facts or mostly fake news?
What ways can we find to understand more?
If we all create our own reality, any breakthroughs?
> Who becomes a "feminazi", bigot, racist, delusion?
> Who sees clearly and who remains in confusion?

Which approaches can lead to oppression?
Racists, sexists, extreme fanatics divide us.
Some must feel superior with no merit, their impression
is to intimidate, unbalance and to deride us.
> Such un-stabilizing people cause many to suffer,
> without adequate services to buffer.

Which approaches lead to progression
in just legislation, responsive institutions?
How do we avoid dogmatic regression?
We zigzag from the center. Slow in restitutions.
> Does knowing have any constants to enhance love?
> Not any savants or discoveries I'm aware of.

213

In the News

Lightning strikes could have sparked life.
Children are beheaded in Mozambique.
Australian Women march against male violence.
Extreme storms devastate many places.

The news every day can be horrific.
Depressed children can't return to school
or attend extracurricular activities except
on-line. Some people balk at wearing masks.

Meetings and gatherings on Zoom.
Relatives can't hug babies. Even
with two Covid shots they can be
infectious. Parents isolated.

Many people will never return
to former jobs. Some workers like
working from home and don't want
to go back to offices. Stores closed.

Size limit to restaurants, order ahead
groceries for pick up. Doctor visits
decree who can come with you. Nursing
homes limit visitors–meet through windows.

These are turbulent times. We destroy
environment and futures. Fossil fuels,
pollution, plastic gyres in oceans. It all
seems overwhelming. We need solutions.

Spring is coming. Buds are forming.
Hearts and minds warming. In lock down,
I ramble room to room, grateful for my
colorful collections of angels and folk art.

I move screen to screen to create, to
get informed and entertained. As long
as my dark chocolate supply lasts, I
can still hope for sweeter days.

April For Renewal?

Ramadan arrived yesterday.
Easter was celebrated on Zoom.
Any suggestions how to display
ideas budding to bloom?
       Isolated, we could not celebrate.
       In bubbles we participate.

Easter was celebrated on Zoom.
Family not gathering this year.
Decorations in an empty room.
I wish guests could appear.
       Flat screens do not compensate.
       We're left to contemplate.

Any suggestions how to display
these celebrations except on screens?
So many issues come into play .
Can we enhance 2D scenes?
       Flat depictions, some sound
       has to do this time around.

Ideas budding to bloom
in this time of introspection.
Uncertainty sure to loom,
provoking deep reflection.
       Hard to comfort from a distance
       to heal this circumstance.

Isolated, we could not celebrate
as a family, new protocols needed.
We must remain separate,
all guidelines heeded.
       We wear masks and limit outings,
       maintain cool and diminish shouting.

In bubbles we participate
in groups of three or four.
Greet great- grandson and elate
we have a group of five once more.
       Love and light bring hope.
       Somehow we'll expand our scope.

Tolkien Reading Day

March 25th is Tolkien Reading Day,
a tribute to The Lord of the Rings.
I also celebrate my 81st birthday.
Frodo Baggins completes his quest, well-springs
       fantasy and imagination to us all.
       I dwell in memories I can recall.

A tribute to The Lord of the Rings
and Tolkien's other fantasy writing–
Oh, the delight this world brings
and the imagination he's igniting.
       I prefer the musings of Ursula LeGuin
       which engages me from deeply within.

I also celebrate my 81st birthday
a white-haired, persistent crone.
Aspects of my situation I display
and share when I am not alone.
       The pandemic keeps me in lock down.
       I struggle to not let it pull me down.

Frodo completes his quest, well-springs
appeals for a dedicated attitude.
Let go and start new beginnings.
Do not forget love and gratitude.
       Tolkien's world still feels very male.
       I prefer more gender equity with female.

Fantasy and imagination to us all
brings possibility and hope.
A chance to explore a new protocol
and options of how to cope.
       A creative exchange I find
       can open and clarify my mind.

I dwell in memories I can recall—
many pivotal experiences and paths.
Sometimes I stumble and fall,
deal with the aftermaths.
       But like Tolkien I enjoy creating worlds,
       and writing down what unfurls.

Coming Ashore

Space junk
came ashore on
the coast. This time
possibly come from a NASA
rocket?

Debris
from Asia and
ships are fairly common.
Fishing gear, garbage dumping in
the sea.

Water
borne discards can
entangle and strangle
creatures, pollute vulnerable
ocean.

Are beach
combers searching
for these objects or just
enjoying the brisk sea breezes?
I watch.

Strange sights
in air, sea, and ground
raise questions, surprises.
More UFO sightings reported.
I look.

Outside
my window I
see dandelions and blue
lupin. Soon I will go outside.
I wait.

A Shovel Poem

Keep life moving forward, looking backward is only for time travelers.
Rachel O. Washington

Keep persisting and resisting.
Life in the pandemic is uncertain.
Moving into a new normal is hard.
Forward into a very turbulent world,
looking with hope beyond pain?
Backward thinking has passed?
Is there a way to stop war and climate change?
Only cock-eyed optimists believe we can.
For most of us we need to feel empowered.
Time to pay attention and act together.
Travelers to anywhere still need masks.

High Five

Each number has certain connections,
meanings which could effect one's perspective?
What are the implications of our selections?
Will we follow a new directive?
      Today I will concentrate on five.
      So many aspects this poem can't give.

Meanings which could effect one's perspective
include the Five of Wands which focuses on self-improvement,
This card suggests challenges, conflicts suggestive
of misunderstanding or poor communication, some movement
      toward resolving these tensions,
      clear the air of apprehensions.

What are the implications of our selections?
Roman symbol for five is X- two crossed hands.
Five senses, five digits on appendages connotations.
Shiva has five faces. Five's meaning expands.
      Universe's five elements: earth, air,water, fire, space.
      Muslims pray five times a days. Islam's five pillars in place.

Will we follow a new directive?
Embrace Chinese five flavors:
sweet, sour, bitter, pungent, salty digestive
tastes a Chinese person favors?
      People born under number five are lucky,
      tend to pursue freedom, need to be plucky.

Today I will concentrate on five.
Five is penta in Latin as in pentagram.
March 25th is my birthday–81 years alive.
How much does five influence who I am?
      Number 5 represents change, uncertainty, realignment,
      inconsistency, freedom, travel–a new assignment?

So many aspects this poem can't give.
Impacts and unknowing are everywhere.
Any guideposts for how we should live?
Numbers for predictions? Astrology? Care?
      These uncertain, dangerous days
      with new twists have been with us always.

Gathering Chi and Shaking Chakras

Late afternoon under overcast sky,
it was a little chilly under the hazelnut
tree. My blue pillow softened my seat.

After a mowing, my two dandelion
companions beside my chair were
gone. Most puffballs poofed.

A few dandelions blew to safety
in the garden. Their bright yellow
blooms like mini-suns.

A small bird with a black head,
gray back and white belly pecks
barkdust near the blooming red azaleas.

Another bluebird hit a nut on the branch
of the apple tree. No bees in the blooms.
No white butterflies appear.

In the distance three different bird calls.
Dogs bark. Mowers moan. No breeze
for wind chimes or pinwheel spins.

All minor distractions from my roiling
mind. After a massage, my muscles
are somewhat relaxed. I breathe deeply.

It is Earth Day. I saw a Greta Thunberg
documentary of her year traveling the world
despite some pandemic roadblocks.

The COVID cases rise in our high risk
state. For a little while, I can reflect
without boundaries and daydream.

Protect the Future

They haul plastic debris from the sea.
Nets and bottles injure wild life,
pollute the oceans with toxins.

The air clogged with satellites,
befouled by belches of our machines.
endangers flights of several species.

The gouged ground, oozes oil.
Filthy rivers flow. Water becomes
more precious for a thirsty planet.

Humanity has not been good stewards.
Their technology has had an impact,
grown beyond our control.

When I sit outside to deep breathe,
what am I breathing in? Was the rain
hazardous to the environment?

So many questions and few answers.
I try to ameliorate my actions to what
I know about. But I know so little.

Too often I feel overwhelmed and worry,
not for myself as much as for children
who face a diminished future.

Preparing for Beltane

The day before Beltane when the veil
between spirituality and physical is thin,
I sit mulling ways to celebrate Beltane.

In the backyard sitting on my blue pillow
under the hazelnut tree and beside a tree
barren of apple blossoms

Wind twerks the wind chimes, jerks
the pinwheel to spin, perks snoozing
flowers, lazing in the sun.

As bugs and bees join with white
butterflies to distract me, I focus
on my options for Beltane tomorrow.

Beltane celebrates the living world,
faces death lovingly, remembers
ancestors in spirit, honors growth,

fertility and life — spring. Some
celebrate as May day, May 1st,
but officially it is May 4th—

the exact cross-quarter date
between the Spring Equinox
and the Summer Solstice.

If one is to celebrate Beltane as a sacred
time, you are encouraged to make it fun
and magical. Traditionally this includes

build a bonfire, dance around a May Pole,
construct a spring altar, craft a ritual for fertility,
transport consciousness into spirit realm.

Through connection with forces of love
and life, you are positively realigned with
the highest possibilities for your future.

Light a Beltane Fire or candle. Beltane
comes from the Gaelic word bealltaninn
which means Blazing Fire. Light a safe fire.

As you gaze into the flames feel the warmth
and elemental power of fire. Symbolically burn away
remnants of stagnant and distorted energy.

I prefer the Candle Magic option. Place candle
on a plate amid Earth elements like twigs, rocks
and crystals. Gaze, vibrate fire energy, cleanse.

Hunt for wildflowers, but do not pick them. Leave
for bees. I sit among 5 buttercups, many puffballs,
dandelions, small purple and yellow flowers.

Celebrate the vibrant life force and energy and
beauty of each. Pause and take a moment to tune
into it. Appreciate color, shape, fragrance, beauty.

Meditate on the forces of life and spring. They
encourage being outside, sitting at the base
of a tree. Close eyes . Breathe deeply. Exhale gently.

I do practice this as often as I can. Tune in and
feel peace, calm and suppleness. Suppleness
is questionable for me. I do chuff chi, rattle chakras.

Celebrate Sacred Sexuality and Sensuality. Eat
strawberries and chocolate, burn incense, anoint
essential oils, align with beautiful blessings in your life.

Leave an offering for the Earth, faeries and nature
spirits. Faeries reside in natural places. You can lure
them to your garden if you respect and protect nature.

Faeries have strong egos and personalities, are
mischievous. If you are treating nature with love and
respect they can bring lightness, playfulness, magic, fun.

They appreciate offerings of honey, crystals, organic sweets
or cakes, fruit and seeds. Faeries do not like large
professions of gratitude, so place offerings quietly.

You can bake a strawberry crisp and enjoy it. I'll
pass on the baking and strawberries. I eat blueberries
and in yogurt for breakfast. Never a strawberry fan.

Spend time in nature. Take a walk or hike. Be fully
present in nature. Look for signs of spring and summer.
Only collect things fallen off plants. Don't disrupt the thriving.

Shake your body. Dance around a May Pole.
Dance to drums. Watch Morris dancers. Shake
your booty, move your hips, dance, skip, jump,

flail your arms, spin, laugh and enjoy. Celebrate life,
spring, sexuality, fertility and magical movement. Release
into the light. Let the old go. Dance to new beginnings.

Be of service towards the Earth and nature. Plant
trees and plants, pick up litter. Start compost heap.
Build a bird house and put out bird seed.

Beltane is a time of abundance of new life, growth,
and fertility. I watch rhododendrons and azaleas
flame along the fence. Muse on vibrant beauty.

Happy 555
    May 5, 2021

Some folks celebrate 555 Day
May (5), day 5, 2021: 2+2+1=5
It is a day to let go, begin new today.
It is a day for us to revive.
        It is a day to look inward.
        It is a day to look forward.

May(5), day 5, 2020:2+2+1=5
Is meaningful for numerologists.
Angel number is for energy change, alive
for an awakening code for mythologists.
        Time to release, transform, transmute.
        Time to give old paradigm patterns the boot.

It is a day to let go, begin new today.
555 is about choice and free will,
support soul path and meaning in a new way.
Focus on your health and highest purpose still.
        Step into Embodied Truth and Light.
        I don't know how to do it right.

It is a day for us to revive.
Rid ourselves of distorted mental constructs.
It is a day for us to thrive.
Get rid of fear, limiting beliefs which obstructs.
        All the old baggage weighs you down.
        Focus on how much you have grown.

It is a day to look inward,
awaken your code, ask for angelic help,
take a step to what your heading toward.
Join in the cosmic yelp.
        You might cleanse with the Violet Flame
        which might help you toward your aim.

It is a day to look forward.
Try some new options, listen to new voices
An energy shift could be your reward.
Awaken, transform journey's choices.
        Who wouldn't want lighten to truth, unblock
        to highest good, to expand and unlock.

World Bee Day

May 20th is the sixth annual World Bee Day.
There is hope for bees if there is clover in
the lawn and when grass is cut every three weeks.

Sponsors hope gardeners take the pledge to not
use quick-release fertilizer, herbicides or pesticides
in the lawn to avoid addiction, soil death.

They claim established lawns should not need
fertilizing. Like grasslands of old they are
capable of taking care of themselves.

We have a chemical-free lawn. Clover and
dandelions can pollinate bees. We have worm-
pecking birds in the yard and pooping creatures.

Since our gardener has a hand-mower, he feels
he has to cut the lawn more often or grass
gets too high to cut. Rare deer and squirrels visit.

Raccoons, nutria and turkey vultures have
not been seen recently. But birds and butterflies
are abundant. Bees nibble blueberry bushes.

Bees stop on the white petals of apple and
strawberries. Bees even sting me. I am a sitting
target. Not the punch of "sting like a bee" Ali.

Flocks of birds fly overhead, few social distance
on the power line. Buttercups flanks march:
west flank south, east flank west. Will they meet?

Many species of birds make noisy flights- quite
the commotion. Rain pelts the yard angels,
activates pinwheel and wind chimes as winds gust.

When a brief period of sun appears, birds settle
and silence. Dog barks muffle. I sit , dry behind
windows and await the episodes of sun.

Towel Day

A towel :"as the most useful thing an interstellar hitchhiker can have" Douglas Adams in The Hitchhikers Guide to the Galaxy

World-wide May 25th is the day to celebrate
the books of Douglas Adams–especially H2G2.
A group called 42 sponsors a global contest
where you can win "Don't panic" towels/bandanas.
Some places give gift cards.

To celebrate Towel Day you can:
1. Carry a towel with you everywhere all day.
2. Read or re-read the books.
3. Listen to radio show or movie adaptations.
4. Hold a H2G2-themed party. Regale guests
    with bad poetry, serve them Pan Galactic Gargle
    Blaster, lots of fish and tea, decorate with Petunias
    and signs urging people not to panic.
5. Attend a local Towel Day event.

During lock down it is not likely we will have many
local parties. I can read or listen about H2G2 and
tuck a towel in my elasticized pants. But I will
choose more appealing meals. Towels are handy
for drying and as napkins. A towel is buttoned
onto my walker which I use more for transporting
things than walking support.

Towel Day is a time to think about absorbing
creativity, celebrating ordinary objects, drying
bodies and tears, wipe up messes. For a little
while a comedy- science fiction perspective
can divert earthly pangs to hope higher.

Sweating It Out

The cloudless blue sky leaves
penetrating heat and light as I
sit in my hot, black, metal chair
in the sun surveying the backyard.

I hear mourning doves and a few
other birdsongs, but they remain hidden.
Lots of white butterflies with erratic flights.
Duos circle in mid air in an aerial dance.

They don't touch, but do they transmit
messages to pass on as they fly in
different directions. Is it like a Butterfly
Express carrying warnings of toxic places?

Crawling in the grass near me with wings
folded is a brownish butterfly or moth.
When it prepares to fly, wings reveal
a dark edge around orangish-brown sections.

The dandelions are gone. Buttercups sprawl
sparsely in the west and abundantly in the east. Now
the yard seems more florally endowed on the west
side. I sit middle yard. Eyes windshield-wiper scene.

The news is filled with Middle East turbulence, fraud,
and Tulsa 1921 massacre centennial. COVID
causes division between masked and unmasked.
Humanity is still a work in progress.

As I sit and begin to sweat in my short sleeves, I
can't roll up my sleeves and get to work. What can
I do with my words to uplift, de-fog minds? My
knees complain as I rise to leave. No charity races.

I have too much time alone and with screens. Now
my backyard sits are getting very warm. Sweat
dampens my body and clothes. Itchy dry skin flakes
scratched from my arm seem to select downfall path.

In all aspects of my life I ponder what to let go and
what to keep. I still sweat the small stuff. I recycle
paper— best of my recycling efforts. My husband uses
the back of my drafts. I prefer a blank page to leave my mark.

Blue Monday

Early afternoon on a drowsy day,
the sun warmed my back as I sat
between hazelnut canopy shadows.

A monarch butterfly flew by my
left shoulder, had it spied my pied,
color-splattered blanket?

I could be a lumpy flower patch perhaps
with new possibilities? Several white
butterflies kept their distance.

A scrub jay flushed from the hazelnut
tree. The trunk blocked my view of
where the jay docked? In underbrush?

A red bug sways a taller grass blade
back and forth. It was too elongated
to be a lady bug and still glistened.

Shadows of birds in the sky whisked
by overhead. Few bird cheeps–not
even usual mourning doves.

Intermittent billowy cloud clusters, dim
sun, but mostly robin's egg blue sky.
My favorite color casts away my blues.

As I ponder the news—ousted Netanyahu,
anti-vaxxers, housing and infrastructure woes...
It is a gift and soul uplift to sit in a thriving place.

Cosmic Connections

Oumaumau–Interstellar Scout

Oumaumau, cosmic cigar
Earthlings ponder what you are.

Comet, asteroid, exo-planet debris.
You look very banged up to me.

Cosmic rays scars and pocks.
How many more mysterious rocks?

Knocked off of a Pluto-like world?
Half of billion years ago unfurled?

N2 ice fragments from exo-planet surface?
Zooming through interstellar space?

Some imaginative folks surmise
you're an alien spacecraft in disguise.

A massive space object flew through
our star system in 2017 with much ado.

Name is Hawaiian for "messenger" or "scout".
What you are leaves some in doubt.

Latest theory you're another's star system's gift
somehow set loose, to galactically drift.

I could not see you, take consensus you are there.
I remain in wonder, delighted you are somewhere.

Space Junk

Space
junk
debris
tossed from
satellites and from
International Space Station.

Crafts
dodge
the waste,
batteries,
huge chunks of junk,
which burns and falls haphazardly.

Space
bound
rockets
all hope to
avoid collisions.
Clunk on people's heads or their homes?

One
fell
in sea–
Atlantic.
Bet fish were impressed.
More crap in ocean plastic gyre.

Do
the
angels
hitchhike, get
impaled or another
dimension? Or unseen, unknown?

Will
we
see
metal stars?
Jagged junk clogging
future routes for Earthling escape?

New
forms
of weird,
benign type
bacteria cling
to ISS? Will seed new planets?

Did
life
spark from
lightning? And
will it end with this
metal pollution sharing space?

Some
day
block sun?
Blinding shine?
I'm uneasy with
chopped Chicken Little drops from sky.

Cosmic Conundrums

NASA's fifth rover Perseverance landed
on Mars, gathering samples, adding
more abandoned metal scars.

Farfarout, the farthest known solar
system object, dwells among
hundreds of billions of stars.

We keep discovering exo-planets
with the hope we detect life and
on Mars perhaps ancient civilizations.

A spacecraft crashed into the Moon
and left the discs of the impenetrable
Lunar library of the history of Earth.

We have sent records into space
before, but this latest is of much
higher technology.

We hope to mine minerals from asteroids,
send robots before we can send flesh. Are
we seeking an escape route from destruction?

We have many theories how people were
seeded on the Earth. We have many more
challenges before we send starseeds.

We speculate on what happened before and
what's to come. How was DNA linked up?
What controls our fate? Anyone know?

If the cosmic code keeps reincarnating me,
I plan to ask more questions before I agree
to another Earth life. Will I have any choice?

What Am I Intended to Do?

What Am I intended to do?
What is the meaning of my existence?
Am I to create a hullabaloo?
Am I to be of assistance or resistance?
      What order guides the multi-verse?
      Just incarnate for better or worse?

What is the meaning of my existence?
Do I come here with a purpose and plan?
Do I come at my own or other's insistence?
Just set adrift to do the best that I can?
      I create my own meaning
      from all the experiences I'm gleaning?

Am I to create a hullabaloo
as a follower or a leader?
A passive wallflower? Paid what's due?
Just an over-population breeder?
      Am I a peacemaker, reformer,
      audience or performer?

Am I to be of assistance or resistance,
a infringer, giver, taker, creator,
lollygag or bloom with persistence?
Am I a detractor, interloper, crafty persuader?
      Do I have any choice in my selections?
      Did I come with pre-determined directions?

What order guides the multi-verse?
Certainly unfathomable forces cooperated?
Are codes enlightened or perverse?
Just not sure how things are operated.
      Am I still to remain in unknowing
      and yet expected to be growing?

Just incarnate for better or worse?
Are we to record Earth's mystery?
Am I to create poetry, prose, or verse?
How can we tell the cosmic story?
      Are we a deluded, transitory, sensory being
      reacting to all the illusions we're seeing?

Dream Ramblers

Do I have a doppleganger in other dimensions?
Am I a multi-dimensional dweller in dreams
to explore alternative intentions?
To explore more possibilities it seems?
> Are nightmares and utopian places
> part of the cosmic interfaces?

Am I a multi-dimensional dweller in dreams
so I can experience other realties?
Or are they also illusions where light beams
on realities and surrealities.
> Do I vary in form and density?
> What is my preferred propensity?

To explore alternative intentions
I drift lightly into the dream state.
I shrug off earthly pretensions
and find other beings to relate.
> Some dreams I remember when waking.
> Some mundane and not earth-shaking.

To explore more possibilities seems
my consciousness travels to spark
my creative constructions in extremes,
bring light to the dark?
> I am aware and am here for limited years.
> Will I shift to other dimensions as it appears?

Are nightmares and utopian places
figments of my imagination or delusional mind?
Will I leave Earth with limited traces?
What in the cosmos will I find?
> Are dreams a preview
> of things I might do?

Part of the cosmic interfaces
could be contact with other sentient beings.
My life and theirs interlaces?
Will I like what I am seeing?
> Whatever the aftermath I seek good dreams
> no matter how improbable this seems.

Last Day of March

When I gaze through the window
into the backyard, a large batch
of purplish-blue lupin catch my eyes.

I am so eager for the chance to sit
outside, unmasked, warm, to inhale
some chi and shake-up my chakrahs.

For a year we have been in lock down—
in Oregon High-Risk category. The news
besides COVID is violent and unjust.

April starts with a Fools Day. We have
plenty of fools, but why give them a
day? Hardly a day to celebrate them.

April is poetry and angel month which
sounds promising and inspiring. I wonder
if angels fear the virus? I doubt it.

But it must be hard to witness so much
suffering on the planet and face such
challenges to support and comfort people.

We hope for light at the end of a dark
tunneling year. We hope love and compassion
will lift away hate and pain. High hopes.

So as I sit at my computer with a space heater
and a stash of dark chocolate, I am hopeful April
is an enlightening poetry month with angels smiling.

A Dream Job

My dreams seem to want me to change jobs.
Abraham Lincoln and I applied for a job
in a bookstore. I told him the job was beneath
him and he was to become President.
I don't know if either of us got the job.

In another attempt at a dream job,
I was at a craft fair and was offered
a job in construction. It was not long
to reveal my incompetence. Soon
I was fired. Dream jobs are hard to keep.

I have ridden many elevators
to many conventions, but I am
not certain my reason to being there.
In the fifth dimension I am as uncertain
as in the third. I'm deluded by illusions.

Here I am teacher, writer and poet mostly.
In my youth I worked in a department store
and as a college guide–not dream jobs but
they were interesting. In my old fogey years
I enjoy creating poetry most–my dream job.

Jumping Layers

If you want to jump layers in time and space you can. You can begin to do this in meditation, trance, dreaming. Later, after you have practiced and understand how to travel in liminal awareness, you travel in different layers of time and space at any time.
Sara Wiseman

Soul journeying, unlimited by time or space
in this lifetime or that lifetime to know
your true self in the flow of the Universe, to embrace
new dimensions, spiritually grow.
    The wonders of sentience, not yours alone
    shared in a multiverse vastly unknown.

In this lifetime or that life time to know
the meaning of your existence,
what lessons to learn as opportunities narrow.
Consciousness continues with persistence.
    How much control or tossed to chance
    in a never-ending cosmic dance?

Your true self in the flow of the universe to embrace
knowledge from expanding sources
can make you feel more complete, race
toward the light not dark resources.
    Jumping layers with your jumping bean soul
    can make many of your fragments whole.

New dimensions spiritually grow
potential options, not just reliance
on the current purloined portfolio
or theories of nescience or science.
    What we believe about faith and doubt
    may never help us figure it out.

The wonders of sentience, not our alone
found in other creatures, probably aliens too.
Communication issues may postpone
connections with species in the Cosmic Zoo.
    Will we fight, ignore or connect?
    So far an impossible prospect.

Shared in a multiverse vastly unknown
is the hopeful chance of a peaceful contact.
Or are we destructive, our future blown?
How will we choose to interact?
    If we jump layers with light, I hope
    we land, don't fall, like when jumping rope.

240

Angel Numbers

When I see triple numbers, I wonder
what angel messages they bring?
What life lessons must I ponder?
A warning or new beginning?
   Yesterday it was 444, today 222.
   I check to see what I'm to do.

What angel messages they bring
usually refer to create and to expand
with the universe, offering
the chance to show love and understand,
   I must proceed with positive thoughts.
   Bring water to emotional droughts.

What life lessons must I ponder?
Each triple number expects me to respond?
Where am I expected to wander?
Are angels a cosmic corresponder?
   Numbers seem to appear at random.
   Where do they really come from?

A warning or a new beginning?
Are the answers found within?
Am I losing or winning?
Should I reflect or just begin?
   Seeing numbers is unnerving.
   What purpose are they serving?

Yesterday it was 444, today 222.
444 urges you trust your wisdom, psychic powers.
A start for a transformation break though?
Will I find a path which empowers?
   222 is to create and to connect,
   promote positive thoughts in your project.

I check to see what I'm to do.
Messages deal with upping energy, motivation.
Begin harmonic, divine duties, to
increase independence, diplomacy, determination.
   You are here to create and expand with universe?
   Am I to do this with my verse?

Space Debris

Space junk falls on Earth when
no longer considered useful.
Most burn up, but other pieces land.

China launched an out of control rocket
which plunked into the Indian Ocean.
For days we worried it would land on us.

How can agencies litter space, cause
objects to dodge when on a distant space
mission? Could we hit a satellite or something?

A ring of space junk orbits the Earth. What is
the limit? We have garbage dumps in the sea.
Now we pollute space as well as land and air.

Imagine when we have gone too far
with our exploitation? Will explorers
from other planets see the ring and leave?

Will they know Earth was then devoid
of life from climate change and reckless
forays into space without a pick-up policy?

It is irresponsible to leave space junk
for others to clean up if we want to survive.
How many planets have died from carelessness?

The pace of space and planetary dumping
increases. Air is less breathable. Mars has
water, but no Earthlings settlers welcome?

Why should we expect any other planets'
inhabitants would want humanity to exploit it?
We need to save ourselves before it is lifeless.

Anywhere Angels Fear to Tread?

What places do angels shun? Do they
have free will whether to intervene?
Do some people not believe in them or pray?
What does being angelic mean?
      If real, we need them very much.
      Are they just a spiritual crutch?

Have free will whether to intervene?
Have moved on to a less stressful planet?
Earth has become a tumultuous scene.
People entangled in the Internet.
      Life overwhelms the sensitive
      and anyone at all pensive.

Do some people not believe in them or pray?
That could not be the reason we feel alone.
How much homage must we pay?
Time's running out for this crone.
      Winged concept a bit fantastical,
      but the lure of angels remains magical.

What does being angelic mean?
A messenger for good? An up-lifter?
Are angels a cosmic go-between?
A guardian? A dimensional shifter?
      What is their role in our lives?
      Trying to see humanity thrives?

If real, we need them very much
If delusional we still wish for them.
We yearn for happiness and such
high notes in our life's anthem.
      Angels can sing and play, some say.
      I like the idea of the angelic way.

Are they just a spiritual crutch?
A way to keep the wayward in line?
Will the vulnerable tend to clutch
to anything that appears divine?
      I choose to believe in angels without proof.
      I just wish they were less distant and aloof.

Heaven Will Never Be The Same

A new arrival appeared at the Pearly Gates
to face four, barefoot, blanched white angels
in non-fitting, sterile gowns, too large wings,
perfectly placed glowing golden halos.

In unison they welcomed the newcomer
and asked what heavenly name she
chose. "Rolenne" The angels gasped.
"But that name is not on our list."

The girl said again, My name will be Rolenne."
Then the transformation began. Rolenne
donned an over-sized, white gown, halo
precisely placed, and shoeless, she moved on.

She leapt cold cloud to cold cloud,
observed angels did not need their
heavy wings with glittery feathers droppings
to fly, but kept them on for tradition.

Harp lessons were part of the angelic
curriculum. Rolenne's now long, wavy
blonde tresses became entangled in
the strings which she plucked with elongated nails.

Her metallic, twangy sound matched the others.
The screechy, piercing sounds lead Rolenne to
declare she wanted to play a trumpet. All
the other angels patiently endured their fate.

The next day Rolenne showed up to harp class
with her hair in a ponytail, fingernails clipped, wings
detached, glistening golden slippers, blue gown belted,
skirt converted to culottes, halo at a rakish angle.

She produced such a melodic tone, effortlessly,
the other angels also rebelled. Angels wore
pants or belted gowns in many patterns, makeup on
diversely colored skin and innovative hairdos.

They even chose a new name. Diversity arrived
in Heaven. Halos expanded to hula hoops or
were tossed in new games. Fashion broke
the mold of earthly perception. Angels were free.

Heaven will never be the same again. Conformity
gives way to creativity. They voice choice, new classes,
and manifest functional garb. Heaven on Earth now
could be an exciting possibility as well as in Heaven.

I Can't Find You, Honey

My mother, nicknamed Honey, always
dressed to the nines when she took
the bus from suburbs to shop in Hartford.

She donned a hat, earrings, make up,
often high boots and her best outfit
for her city excursions.

In my dream I am shopping in a department
store in Hartford. I am about to get on
an escalator when I see her.

She wears a broad-brim hat to match
a reddish-purple pant suit with boots. Very chic.
I call to her and we are about to board.

The escalator has a flat platform with four
chairs. Two were taken. After some trouble
to sit down, she asks me why I came.

I am taking a break from teaching. The two
of us browse around and somehow we
become separated. I can not find her.

I move like a gazelle. My bone on bone
knees are healed in this time warp. Lost,
I fall to the floor and weep with deep grief.

It feels so real, but when I wake up I know
I would not find her then or now. A profound
sadness overcomes me–stuck in this reality.

Levitating

Last night I was in a college dorm.
The rooms were all a mess. In the hallway
arms at my side, I slowly levitated several
times, head hits ceiling and I come down.

I was a younger me and enjoyed the trip
up and own. When I woke up, I researched
the meaning of levitating in dreams.
It is a positive meaning in most cases.

It indicates someone with quirky and
unusual thoughts who powers through
to reach one's goals. You are supported.
You face challenges and remain strong.

Through the day I carry the image of
me in the hallway and recall the one semester
I was able to live on campus to get
the college experience and not commute.

In 1959 the dorms were overcrowded.
Four girls with two bunk beds, two dressers,
two desks, two closets. Obviously a room
for two. After that experience I was glad

to commute with my father, wait at my
grandmother's next to college, drink hot
chocolate until my father drove me home.
I never wanted to attended that college.

I had dreams of Columbia in NYC which
my parents could not afford and they thought
it was too dangerous. I graduated in 3 1/2 years,
married, then went to graduate school.

My dream indicated I was happy with the
trashy dorm? No, it must have some deeper
meaning. I'm rising above some problem?
Perhaps unresolved disappointment?

I go crazy places in my dreams–different
dimensions and some dreams therapeutic.
But this one from over 60 years ago puzzles me.
Am I on track? Sharing quirky ideas effectively?

Super Full Moon

Tonight I want to swoon at the cool moon
after a 81 degree sit in my backyard. Very
few clouds tonight for a clear view?

The butterfly circle dance is short. Two
blue jays in an open garden patch, a brief
beak to beak, then flop to sun or dump.

The red roses flush their color. The grass
still uneven. Three tall dandelions with
some unopen blooms, like a chandelier.

I was about to shift to shade, as I felt
like I was frying, when I decide to go
inside. Everything looked so normal.

The headlines reveal an apartment building
collapse in Miami, politicians tug of war,
local to world-wide tragedies. I tend to skim.

The discovery of older and more diverse bones,
make us reconsider our origins and where we
are in this chain of sentient beings.

Our ancestors seem more clever than we give
them credit. How they diversified is unknown.
The face on the moon–reflecting another branch?

When I gaze at that cold, barren moon, I am happy
I am very warm in a changing green habitat, chugging
chakras and inhaling sunshine, like my ancestors.

Poems Published Elsewhere

Cloud Followers in The Advocate

In Summer 2021 of Pen Women Newsletter
   Breaking Free
   Becoming Anti-Social

Other Books by Linda Varsell Smith

Cinqueries: A Cluster of Cinquos and Lanternes
Fibs and Other Truths
Black Stars on a White Sky
Poems That Count
Poems That Count Too
*Winging-It: New and Selected Poems
*Star Stuff: A Soul-Splinter Experiences the Cosmos
*Light-Headed: A Soul-Splinter Experiences Light
*Sparks: A Soul-Splinter Experiences the Cosmos
*Into the Clouds: Seeking Silver Linings
*Mirabilia: Manifesting Marvels, Miracles and Mysteries
*Spiral Hands: Signs of Healing
*Lacunae: Mind the Gap
*Wayfinding: Navigating the Unknown
*Hugger-Muggery: Ways to Hugs and Mugs
*The Ground Crew: Beings with Earthly Experiences
*Waves: Ebbs and Flows
*Grounded with Gaia: Bonded with Earth
*Changes in Climate: Cleaning the Atmosphere
*Beyond Windows: 2020 Aperatures
*Curves: 2020 Swervings Second Half of 2020
*Angels Encore: An Anthology of Angel Poems
        * Available at www. Lulu.com/spotlight/rainbowcom

Chapbooks:
Being Cosmic, Light-headed, Intra-space Chronicles, Red Cape Capers

On-Line Website Books:
free access *RainbowCommunications.org*
Syllables of Velvet, Word-Playful, Poetluck

Anthologies: Poets Ponder Photographs, Poetic License, Poet
License 2015, The Second Genesis, Jubilee, The Eloquent
Umbrella

Twelve novels in the Rainbow Chronicle Series.